THE ROYAL
HISTORICAL SOCIETY
1868-1968

By

R. A. HUMPHREYS

LONDON
OFFICES OF
THE ROYAL HISTORICAL SOCIETY
UNIVERSITY COLLEGE LONDON, GOWER STREET, W.C.1
1969

Made and printed in Great Britain by
Butler & Tanner Ltd, Frome and London

CONTENTS

PREFACE

I wish to express my gratitude to Mr C. W. Crawley for making available to me passages relating to the Royal Historical Society from the diary of Sir George Prothero; to Sir Eric Fletcher, the President of the Selden Society, for copies of the Selden Society's minutes; to Mrs Margaret Sharp, for allowing me to see and to cite the papers of her father, the late Professor T. F. Tout; to Professor R. W. Southern, the Literary Executor of Sir Maurice Powicke, for permission to make use of the letters written by Sir Maurice to Professor H. Hale Bellot; and to Professor Bellot himself, both for lending me these letters and for allowing me to draw on his own long memories of the Society.

The Royal Historical Society is the heir and representative of the Camden Society, which was founded in 1838 and was amalgamated with the Royal Historical Society in 1897. A brief account of the Camden Society was written by the late Charles Johnson in 1938 and published in 1940. It is reprinted, with a few omissions and some small verbal emendations, in Appendix I. The omissions are indicated by three dots and the original notes by the initials C.J. A few additional notes have been provided by Mr. A. T. Milne. To him, and to those many other of my colleagues who have assisted me with their advice, I tender my warmest thanks.

R. A. H.

THE ROYAL HISTORICAL SOCIETY

1868–1968[1]

The Royal Historical Society was founded at a meeting held on 23 November 1868 at Somerset Chambers, 151 The Strand. The first paper read to it was given by Dean Hook[2] on 'Marlborough and his battles' on 24 May 1869, when Sir John Bowring took the chair. The first President, George Grote, then President of University College and Vice-Chancellor of the University of London, was elected on 6 January 1870; and the first volume of the Society's *Transactions* was issued in two parts in 1871 and 1872. In 1872, also, at the instance of the second President, Earl Russell,[3] the Society was granted the style of a 'royal' society.

The presiding genius, if genius is the word, over these early years of the Society was the Rev. Dr Charles Rogers.[4] Rogers was a Scottish Presbyterian clergyman, a journalist, a hymnologist and a genealogist, whose writings fill five columns in the catalogue of the British Museum. An unsuccessful candidate for the Chair of Ecclesiastical History in the University of St Andrews, where he was educated, and an honorary doctor of laws of Columbia, he had been for several years chaplain to the garrison of Stirling Castle. He had acted also as secretary to two committees concerned with the raising of funds for the erection of a memorial to the Scottish national hero, William Wallace. The dissensions,

[1] The Presidential Address, 6 December 1968.
[2] Walter Farquhar Hook (1798–1875), dean of Chichester.
[3] Lord John Russell.   [4] 1825–90.

1

perhaps unavoidable, to which these last activities gave rise, a libel suit, and the failure of a weekly journal, the *Stirling Gazette*, which he had launched, all contributed to his bankruptcy in 1863 and to his resignation from the chaplaincy. Deprived 'both of living and estate',[1] and pursued by unhappy accusations of self-interest or sharp practice, he shook the dust of Scotland from his feet and retired to England, where he founded the Naval and Military Tract Society, with himself as general secretary, in 1865,[2] and the Grampian Club, for 'the editing and printing of works illustrative of Scottish literature, history, and antiquities', with himself as general editor, on 2 November 1868.[3]

Associated with Rogers in the establishment of the Grampian Club, and its first secretary, was a much younger man, Louis Charles Alexander.[4] A Scotsman, like Rogers, and an ex-chairman of the Glasgow Athenaeum, Alexander was a member of the accountancy firm of Alexander, Gibson and Rae. He later made for himself a career in banking and insurance, and this he combined with a taste for foreign travel and the writing of short stories and essays—*The Book*

[1] Charles Rogers, *Leaves from my Autobiography* (London, 1876), p. 203. On the Wallace monument project and Rogers' part in it see H. J. Hanham's essay on 'Mid-Century Scottish Nationalism: Romantic and Radical', in Robert Robson, ed., *Ideas and Institutions of Victorian Britain: Essays in honour of George Kitson Clark* (London, 1967), pp. 143–79.

[2] *Autobiography*, pp. 227, 234; and see his pamphlet, *The Serpent's Track: A Narrative of Twenty-Two Years Persecution* (London, 1880), pp. 16–17. The Society continued an earlier institution which Rogers had founded in Scotland in 1862 under the name of The British Christian Institute.

[3] He had in mind, he says, the examples of the Bannatyne Club at Edinburgh (1823–61), the Maitland Club at Glasgow (1828–59), and the Spalding Club at Aberdeen (1839–71). *Autobiography*, p. 331. The Club issued 23 vols. between 1869 and 1891, a number of them by Rogers.   [4] 1839–1913.

of Ballynoggin (in dialect), for example, in 1902, and *Echoes of Whistler* in 1910.

It was in Alexander's offices, or, rather, in those of Alexander, Gibson and Rae, that the inaugural meeting of the Society was held. Apart from the three members of the firm, the only other persons present were Dr Rogers, Dr J. E. Carpenter (who does not otherwise appear in the records of the Society, even by the payment of a subscription) and the Rev. Samuel Cowdy,[1] a Baptist minister in charge of the Arthur Street Chapel, Camberwell Road, and the author of *Sunny Poesy* (1867) and *Heavenward Ho, or, Story Coxen's Log* (1873). Dr Rogers presided. A constitution and laws for 'the Royal Historical Society of Great Britain', markedly similar to those of the Grampian Club adopted three weeks earlier, were read and approved. The objects of the Society were defined as the 'conducting of Historical, Biographical and Ethnological investigations'. Regular meetings were to be held. The entrance fee was fixed at three guineas and the subscription rate at two, though the founders were to pay one guinea only and no entrance fee at all. The Archbishop of York, William Thompson, whose reputation had been so early established by his *Outlines of the Laws of Thought*, was designated President, and among the 'noblemen and gentlemen of eminence' proposed as Vice-Presidents and members of Council were to be found, besides the names of three peers and one bishop, those of Thomas Carlyle, George Grote, J. A. Froude, Dean Stanley[2] and Sir John Bowring. Dr Rogers was appointed Historiographer and Louis Charles Alexander Secretary, with a salary of £100 a year and ten per cent of the Society's receipts from all sources until his income should amount to £300.

---

[1] 1817–1900. Cowdy was a member of Council till Nov. 1873.

[2] Arthur Penrhyn Stanley (1815–81), dean of Westminster.

A second meeting took place on 8 February 1869, when letters were read, approving the objects of the Society, not only from the Archbishop, Grote, Froude and Bowring, but from Dean Hook, John Ruskin and Earl Russell as well, though not from Thomas Carlyle. Still further letters were read on 19 April,[1] this time from Dean Stanley, Sir John Lubbock[2] and Sir Roundell Palmer,[3] among others, but, again, not from Thomas Carlyle. This epistolary benediction, it may be thought, is slender justification for the pre-eminent position among the Society's founders accorded to some of these distinguished persons in the preamble to the Royal Charter of Incorporation twenty years later. But all of them lent it at least their moral support, and some of them their financial support, and all, except the Archbishop, allowed their names to grace the list of the Society's Council. The Archbishop, however, plainly declined the presidency, and for the first year the infant Society, though it listened to a number of papers and elected a number of Fellows, including, as an Honorary Fellow, the American Minister in London, John Lothrop Motley, managed without a President at all. Not till the first Annual General Meeting on 6 January 1870 was an election held, and the choice then fell on Grote. Failing him, the office was to be offered to Russell,

---

[1] The meeting of 8 Feb. was held at 2 Paul's Alley, 51 Paternoster Row, that of 19 April and four subsequent meetings in May, June and July took place at 2 Falcon Court, Temple Chambers, 32 Fleet Street, the chambers to which Alexander had moved and which were the offices not only of the Historical Society but of the Grampian Club and the Provincial Record Association. No. 2 Paul's Alley was occupied in the 1870's by Henry Wright, publisher, who had been nominated as the first Treasurer of the Society. His offices were at 65 Paternoster Row in 1868 and it is not clear when he left there. He attended none of the Society's meetings.

[2] First Baron Avebury, 1834–1913.

[3] First Earl of Selborne, 1812–95.

Froude or Ruskin. In a letter to Rogers on 14 January Grote accepted it in the following terms:[1]

> Sir,—I beg to acknowledge your letter of the 12th, informing me that the Historical Society of Great Britain have done me the honour to elect me president of the Society for the present session. If this post entailed the necessity of any duties or attendances, I should be compelled respectfully to decline it, for my time is already fully occupied with other engagements. But as you assure me that I shall be 'held fully exempted from duties of every kind', I willingly consent that my name should appear as you have placed it among the very distinguished names of your printed list.—I have the honour to be, Sir, your obedient humble Servant,
>
> Geo. Grote.

While the Society thus gained its first President, it lost its first Secretary. The minutes of the Annual General Meeting record that five persons, and five persons only, were present, including Rogers and Alexander. It was agreed not only to elect Grote as President at the head of a distinguished list of Vice-Presidents and Councillors, but that a volume of Transactions should be published, funds permitting, before the end of the session, and that permission should be sought for the use of the prefix 'royal', improperly assumed in the first draft of the Society's constitution but thereafter abandoned. Rogers intimating that the Treasurer,[2] who had been Treasurer only in name, had retired, a new one was appointed.[3] Alexander, who had paid the requisite fee of twenty

[1] Rogers, *Autobiography*, p. 352.

[2] Henry Wright, of the firm of Houlston and Wright, publishers and booksellers. There is no evidence that he ever exercised the functions of treasurer.

[3] Alfred Gliddon, manager of the City Bank, Tottenham Court Road, in whose premises the meeting was held.

guineas, was elected a life-member, received the 'best thanks' of the Society 'for his munificence' in making a donation of £50, which Rogers announced, and declared that his numerous engagements prevented his continuance as Secretary. The meeting thereupon resolved that he should be formally thanked 'for his founding the Society and for his diligence and zeal in promoting its success', and nominated as his successor, though in an honorary, not a paid, capacity, Thomas Laurence Kington-Oliphant,[1] of Balliol and the Inner Temple. It also passed the extraordinary resolution that, an assurance having been received 'from Mr Alexander, that he held Mr Oliphant and the other Members free of all legal responsibility connected with the matter', the proceedings of a meeting held on 10 December (of which no minutes exist) should be cancelled, save for the election of two Fellows.

Such is the record, and the record is wrong.[2] Alexander was not present at the meeting. He had not made a donation of £50 to the Society, at least not in the sense that the minutes imply; he had foregone the half of the salary still owed to him.[3] And while he had given up the secretaryship, the reason was not pressure of engagements, or at least not that alone. It is best given in his own words.[4] 'Dr Rogers,' he wrote in 1881, 'taking advantage of my absence in Devonshire (of which he was well aware) came to my office, made some disingenuous pretext to my clerk, and

---

[1] 1831–1902. Author of a *History of Frederick the Second, emperor of the Romans* (1862), *The Old and Middle English* (1878) and *The New English* (1886), etc.

[2] The Society's Minute Book, kept by Rogers, covering the years 1868–78, contains fair copies of the minutes only, and only those of the meeting of 23 Nov. 1868 are properly attested.

[3] Subscription Book, 29 April 1869–31 Oct. 1881.

[4] Alexander to [W. Herbage], 18 May 1881. R[oyal] H[istorical] S[ociety Archives], H.3/1/2.

removed the box containing all the books and papers relating to, and belonging to this Society, as also that of the Grampian Club. On my return I addressed myself to the police, and instructed my solicitor to take proceedings against him.[1] Then he came to me and made a strong appeal that I should not ruin the Societies by legal (criminal) proceedings, and so forth—very much after his kind. Equally after his kind, he had some "meetings" of Committee. It is *possible* that one or two of his friends attended: but I know that he has certain free and independent ideas on such matters. . . I was however induced—weakly, perhaps—to accept the excuses, humbly enough made, which were showered on me and— tired of the continual appeals, and disgusted with both the unscrupulousness of the act and the subsequent abasement by which it was attempted to excuse it and to procure my cessation of proceedings—I gave up the Secretaryship'.

So ended the first crisis in the history of the Society, and so began what Alexander called the 'long years of Rogerian control'. The minutes, this time correctly as well as eloquently, reveal the consolidation of the Historiographer's position. He was elected a life-member and exempted from all payments to the Society's funds (to which, in fact, he had contributed nothing) in January 1872. An annual stipend of £20 was awarded to him in April and raised to £120 in November. In November, also, Kington-Oliphant apparently having resigned—there is no explanation or even notice of this[2]—the Historiographer quietly assumed the

---

[1] This seems to explain a curious minute of 24 Feb. 1871: 'It was agreed to pay £6.12.6 being half of Messrs Crawley, Arnold and Green's account in the case of the Society and the late Secretary'.

[2] In the draft *Report of Secretary and Treasurer presented to the Council on Thursday, 14 March 1878* (R.H.S., H.3/1/4), Rogers (who wrote most of it) stated both that he had discharged the duties of Secretary since Nov. 1869 and that he had been Acting Secretary since

office of Honorary Secretary. In May 1873 Council resolved to co-operate with a committee which had been set
up to procure, by public subscription, and in recognition of
his literary and public services, the erection of a house for Dr
Rogers,[1] and to recommend this undertaking to the Fellows.
In the following November his salary was raised to £150,
and he received a gratuity of £340, by way of compensation
for his unpaid labours between 1868 and 1872.[2] A year later
his salary was again raised, this time to £200, and again, in
November 1875, to £300, when he was also given an allow-
ance of £20 as Secretary. A further gratuity of 100 guineas
followed in February 1876 and a final increase of his salary
to £420 nine months later.

These were substantial rewards to be gained from a young
society not yet ten years old. But no one can deny the zeal
with which Rogers promoted the interests of an institution
whose financial welfare coincided so closely with his own.
The Society had begun its second financial year, in January
1870, with a balance of 4s. 9d, and a membership of some 48
or 50 persons, including associates,[3] honorary members and
corresponding members. In February this number was
raised to 60 by an amalgamation with the Provincial Record

Jan. 1870. In *The Serpent's Track*, p. 50, he implies that Kington-
Oliphant was Honorary Secretary in name only. The Secretary and
Treasurer's report, much edited, appears as the *Report of the Council*,
bound into *Transactions*, vii (1878).

[1] This was Grampian Lodge, Forest Hill, of which the foundation
stone seems already to have been laid by George Cruikshank, the
artist and an Honorary Fellow. *Autobiography*, p. 366.

[2] Equivalent, that is, to £100 p.a. from Nov. 1868 to Nov. 1873,
less £160 already paid to him.

[3] The class of Associates was provided for in the first draft of the
Society's Constitution, but does not appear in the revised version,
approved in Nov. 1870. But Associates certainly existed, and are
referred to from time to time in the 1870's.

Association, an institution which Rogers later described as 'got up, with a view of carrying out in some measure the work since undertaken by the Royal Commission on Historical Manuscripts',[1] and which was, in fact, one more of his children. It was now also decided to invite 'persons of literary mark and position to become members of the Society', and the Historiographer, already exercising the functions of Secretary, wrote to 400 such persons. The results were disappointing. The subscription was therefore reduced to a guinea, with half a guinea entrance fee, and Rogers, in November, was able to announce that 27 persons had agreed to be enrolled, including both A. W. Ward and H. C. Maxwell Lyte.[2]

Meanwhile, through the President, the Society had approached the Home Secretary, Henry Austin Bruce, later, as Lord Aberdare, himself to become President of the Society, for permission to use the appellation 'royal'. In a letter of 31 March, which Grote described as 'not unreasonable', Bruce replied that it would be 'better to defer laying before the Queen the Petition of the Society for the proposed mark of Her Majesty's approbation until by its published Works and actual performance the Society has established a claim to such a recognition of its usefulness'.[3] Highly approving, so it said, of these 'suggestions', Council decided to renew the application when the membership had reached 100 and the first part of the Transactions had been published.[4]

This appeared in February 1871, followed by a second

---

[1] Draft *Report of Secretary and Treasurer . . . Thursday, 14 March 1878.* The Association consisted of some ten or twelve local antiquaries, three of whom were sufficiently distinguished to find a place in the *Dictionary of National Biography.*

[2] Minutes, 10 Feb., 22 June, 24 Nov. 1870. Neither Ward nor Lyte maintained their membership continuously.

[3] *Ibid.,* 22 June 1870.

[4] *Ibid.,* 24 Jan. 1871.

part in 1872. The two parts contained, according to Rogers, 'the Society's Transactions during its first two sessions, 1869–70 and 1870–71'.[1] This they certainly did not do, for some papers which had been read were not included and some which were included had not been read. There were, however, no less than four contributions by Rogers himself, accounting for more than half the volume, and gratifyingly enough, he was able to report, after the appearance of Part I, that he had received 'a number of communications highly approving of the same'.[2] The renewed application to the Home Secretary, however, was still deferred, even though the membership had reached 100 by the end of the year. Grote had died in June, and Russell, a Vice-President, who agreed to succeed him, did not take office till November. But the renewed application was made through Russell in the following year, and this time with success.

Russell's first and last appearance before the Society was on 24 June 1872, when he delivered an inaugural address. He was nearly eighty and had not been well, 'though he felt better', he said, 'since he came into the room' and 'always rejoiced to be at the post of duty'. Of the address itself, it is sufficient to say, with one of his successors, that it was 'admirably brief'.[3] Russell was not, like Grote, who never

---

[1] For the re-edition of this volume see A. T. Milne, ed., *A Centenary Guide to the Publications of the Royal Historical Society 1868–1968 and of the former Camden Society 1838–1897* (London, 1968), pp. vii–viii.

[2] Minutes, 24 Feb. 1871.

[3] T. F. Tout, Presidential Address, 11 Feb. 1926, *Transactions*, 4th ser., ix (1926), p. 6. Russell's address is in *ibid.*, ii (1873), pp. 9–14. The 'room' was the Scottish Corporation Hall, Crane Court, Fleet Street, where the Society met from Feb. 1871 to April 1874. The meetings in 1870 had been at the Treasurer's residence, the City Bank, 159–160 Tottenham Court Road. Russell failed, in 1873, to secure accommodation for the Society, through the First Commissioner of Works, in Somerset House. It moved, in May 1874, to the Medical

addressed the Society at all, a great historian. But, in the world at large, the name of 'glorious John' carried immense prestige, and the Society no doubt reaped the benefit both of this and of its new title. In November, 158 persons were elected Fellows at a single meeting of Council—an 'extraordinary accession', as Rogers rightly observed, which he ascribed to three causes, 'the recognition of the Society as "Royal" by Her Majesty the Queen', 'the popularity of the new President', and, less credibly, 'a general satisfaction with the first volume of the Society's Transactions'.[1] Further accessions resulted from amalgamations with the English Reprint Society in 1874 and the British Genealogical Institute in 1876—both of them infant societies and both, curiously enough, enjoying the services of Dr Rogers as secretary.[2] And throughout Russell's presidency, which ended only with his death in May 1878, the membership of the Society, even when the subscription rate had again been raised,[3] continued to grow.[4]

Who were the members? For the most part they seem to have been drawn, naturally enough, from the professional classes. They included clergymen and physicians, army-officers and civil servants, barristers and solicitors, bank-

---

Society's rooms, 11 Chandos Street, Cavendish Square, to Dr Williams's Library, 16 Grafton Street East, in June 1878, to the Royal Asiatic Society's rooms, 22 Albemarle Street, in Nov. 1879, back to the Medical Society's rooms in Nov. 1882, and to the Royal Medical and Chirurgical Society's rooms at 20 Hanover Square in Sept. 1890.

[1] Minutes, 26 Nov. 1872.

[2] The English Reprint Society, founded in 1873, had 57 members, of whom 26 were already Fellows of the Royal Historical Society; the British Genealogical Institute, founded in Nov. 1875, had about 24.

[3] To two guineas for new members only, with an entrance fee of three. Minutes, 13 April 1876.

[4] The number of ordinary Fellows reached 544 in Nov. 1878 as compared with 500 in Nov. 1877 and 520 in Nov. 1879.

B

managers, journalists, engineers, teachers. Among a sprinkling of peers and country gentlemen they included, also,
women. 'I hold that a society without ladies', said Dr
Rogers, 'is like a garden without flowers'.[1] A few were
Fellows of the Royal Society: B. W. Richardson, the President of the Medical Society of London, who acted as
President or Chairman of Council—an office instituted in
1876; James Heywood, a former M.P. and a pioneer of the
Free Library movement, who was also a Chairman; and the
mining engineer, Thomas Sopwith, a Vice-Chairman, are
examples. And a number, of course, were men of letters,
writers on history and genealogy, and antiquaries.

Few, however, at least of those who attended the Society's
meetings, could properly be described as professional historians, if, indeed, such a category as yet existed. The Society
was not, in any real sense, a professional society. And its
standards were not professional standards. Its beginnings
coincided with important developments both at Oxford and
Cambridge. William Stubbs had been elected to the Regius
Professorship of Modern History at Oxford in 1866, the
same year in which A. W. Ward was appointed Professor of
History and of English Language and Literature at Owen's
College, Manchester; and a separate School of Modern History was established at Oxford in 1871. At Cambridge,
where history, in Ward's view, had been treated as 'an
agreeable *parergon*',[2] the Historical Tripos was created in

---

[1] 24 April 1879. *Transactions*, viii (1880), p. 387. The first woman
member was Lady Bowring, elected an Honorary Fellow in 1872. The
first paper read by a woman was given by Miss Helen Taylor, an
Associate, on 13 Feb. 1879. Miss Rose Graham and Miss Eleanor
Lodge were the first women members of Council, in 1919 and 1924
respectively. The *Report of Secretary and Treasurer* in 1878 stated that
'From the commencement Lady Associates have been admitted'. But
they were not always so called.

[2] 'The Study of History at Cambridge' [1872], *Collected Papers:*

1873.[1] T. F. Tout, J. H. Round, Richard Lodge, R. L. Poole, C. H. Firth, were all undergraduates at Balliol in the 1870's. At Cambridge, in these years, G. W. Prothero and William Cunningham, later to be joined by F. W. Maitland, had begun to teach. Of these men no less than five, in addition to Ward himself, were to become Presidents of the Society. But though Ward became a Fellow in 1870 and Stubbs an Honorary Fellow in 1878, the Society, in the 1870's, was divorced from the currents of thought which were beginning to work a transformation in historical studies at Oxford and Cambridge and were soon to do so at Manchester. Its affairs were conducted by a small group of persons, none of whom was attuned to these ideas. The average attendance at the ordinary meetings of Council in the seven years from 1870 to 1878 was four, of whom Dr Rogers was always one. Papers were read to more numerous gatherings. The nucleus of a library was formed, at first housed in the Medical Society's rooms (where the Society was then meeting) in Chandos Street.[2] The Society, Rogers could boast in 1877,[3] 'has arranged to exchange *Transactions* with nearly every Historical Society in Europe and with the principal Historical Societies of America,[4] and the Kings of Belgium and

---

Historical, Literary, Travel and Miscellaneous (5 vols., Cambridge 1921), v, p. 250.

[1] Jean O. McLachlan, 'The Origin and Early Development of the Cambridge Historical Tripos', *Cambridge Historical Journal*, ix (1947–1949), pp. 78–84.

[2] It was removed to Dr Williams's Library in Grafton Street in 1877 (before the Society itself moved there), afterwards following the Society's peripatetic career till put in store, for lack of other accommodation, in 1884.

[3] Rogers to Thomas Sopwith, 23 May 1877. R.H.S., H.3/1/1.

[4] He visited the United States in the summer of 1880 and proposed to lecture, on his return, on 'The Historical Societies of America, derived from personal examination and inquiry'.

Sweden[1] have, through their prime ministers, accepted honorary membership'. An interesting step, of which no more was to be heard, was the appointment of local secretaries, in 1876, in various English towns, and, overseas, in Belfast, Dublin and Lima.[2] In 1876, also, Council decided to institute two prizes for the encouragement of the study of history at the Art Training School in South Kensington and at the Birkbeck Literary and Scientific Institution,[3] and this was followed, in 1880–1, by a course of lectures on the science of history, delivered at South Kensington by the Hungarian refugee, Gustavus George Zerffi, who became Chairman of Council in December 1880.[4] But the successive volumes of *Transactions*, which Rogers edited, showed little improvement over the first volume, and the Society found itself saddled in 1876 with a Genealogical Section, which Rogers invented (with a separate subscription)[5] and whose sole justification seems to have been the publication of four of his own works. It should be added, as a financial pendant to these literary activities, that not a penny of the Society's funds was invested and that the Historiographer's salary, in the late 1870's, absorbed more than a half of the current receipts.

The critics of this state of affairs first made themselves heard in Council in January 1878, when a letter was read

---

[1] Joined, in the same year, by the Emperor and Empress of Brazil and General Grant.

[2] Minutes, 9 Nov. 1876.

[3] *Ibid.*, 14 Dec. 1876.

[4] For Zerffi see A. D. Momigliano, 'Da G. G. Zerffi a Ssu-ma Ch'ien', *Revista Storica Italiana*, lxxvi (1964), pp. 1058–69.

[5] Minutes, 10 Feb. 1876. This was on the amalgamation with the British Genealogical Institute, which Rogers and some of his friends had established in Nov. 1875. The Section disappeared when Rogers himself disappeared.

from G. L. (afterwards Sir George) Gomme,[1] 'a clerk, I believe, in the Board of Works, as well as an industrious contributor to *Notes and Queries*', so Rogers described him. It complained that membership was too cheaply obtained, that the annual statement of accounts was unsatisfactory, that compounded subscriptions were not invested, and that only one volume was published a year. The Society, said Gomme, was 'spoken of amongst literary circles with anything but respect'.[2] Council took no notice of this communication, though it did instruct the Secretary and Treasurer to draw up a report on the Society's financial position and later agreed that every effort should be made to produce the annual volume from the funds of the current year and that thereafter a sum equal to the life-subscriptions should be invested.[3] The question of the Society's financial condition, however, was again raised at the Annual General Meeting in November, when the former Home Secretary, H. L. Bruce, now Lord Aberdare, presided—Aberdare had succeeded to the presidency on the death of Russell. And not only was it raised at the Annual General Meeting; it was raised, more publicly, in the pages of the *Athenaeum*.[4]

At this point Council was so foolish as to propose a by-law which would have empowered it to expel from the Society any member it pleased for such cause as it deemed sufficient without the necessity of explanation, and to allow the Secretary to send out a circular stating that a 'medal or decoration', 'suited for evening dress', or for displaying 'at *fêtes* or other public celebrations', had been designed and could be worn. A withering paragraph at once appeared in

---

[1] 1853–1916. Clerk to the London County Council, 1900–14, and a founder of the Folk-lore Society. Knighted, 1911.

[2] Printed Circular, signed by Rogers, 15 Dec. 1880.

[3] Minutes, 10 Jan., 14 Nov. 1878.

[4] 7, 28 Dec. 1878 (H. L. Michelsen).

the *Athenaeum*. 'These aids to historical research', it re-
marked, 'cost two guineas if of silver, and six when of
gold.'[1] Angry letters followed from H. H. (later Sir Henry)
Howorth,[2] himself a recently elected member of Council,
and others, protesting against these 'grotesque proceedings',
and also against the sums 'most profusely' granted to the
Secretary, the undignified recruiting of Fellows, and the
poor quality of the Society's publications.[3]

The President now felt constrained to hold a special
meeting of Council and himself put forward suggestions
for the reform of the Society's administration.[4] The obnox-
ious by-law had already been withdrawn. No more, it was
agreed, should be heard of the medals, and more business-
like methods were to be introduced into the Society's proceedings. It may be doubted whether this intention was
realised, though the excuse for Rogers' shortcomings in this
respect, advanced by one of his supporters, is not wholly
convincing: 'He is essentially a literary man; and literary
men are seldom perfect accountants, or good men of business'.[5] But Council was no longer the docile body of earlier
days, attended by three or four persons only. An opposition
to the Secretary had formed within it; its members were
defeated in their efforts to secure a reform of the Society's
rules and regulations[6] and angered by Rogers' attempts to

---

[1] Minutes, 9 Jan., 13 Feb. 1879; *Athenaeum*, 15 March 1879. Fellows
could already buy a diploma for 6s.

[2] 1842–1923. K.C.I.E., 1892; F.R.S., 1893; M.P. for South Salford,
1886; author of a *History of the Mongols* (3 vols., London, 1876–
1888).

[3] *Athenaeum*, 22 March, 5 April, 3 May 1879 (Howorth); 29 March
(H. Fishwick); 12 April, 3 May (J. C. Cox); 12 April (H. E. Michelsen).

[4] Scroll Minutes, 21 May 1879. Also 12 June, 10 July.

[5] Minutes, 18 March 1880.

[6] *Ibid.*, 3 Nov., 18 Dec. 1879; Statement by General Allan, 18 Dec.
1879. R.H.S., H.3/1/2.

silence his critics;[1] and in November one at least of them sought the aid of the press. An inspired article in the *Athenaeum* took the Society severely to task for the mismanagement of its affairs, implying not only that its revenue was declining but that it was already in debt;[2] and this was followed, in January 1880, by an advertisement inviting Fellows who disapproved of the Secretary's conduct to join together in an appeal to the President.[3] Rogers, who already had at least two libel suits on hand, began an action against the *Athenaeum*'s publisher,[4] himself publishing also an extraordinary pamphlet, *The Serpent's Track. A Narrative of Twenty-Two Years Persecution.* In stormy sessions of Council the opposition in vain tried to secure a reduction of his salary and to bring him to book in other ways.[5] At the Annual General Meeting in November, his supporters contrived to put forward a new list of Councillors, from which his critics' names were excluded. The meeting, however, rejected the list, refused to adopt the Annual Report, and by the casting vote of the Chairman, Aberdare himself, referred it to a Committee of Enquiry, then and there appointed, while the meeting stood adjourned.[6]

Admitting that the Society's revenues had diminished and that it was, in fact, in debt, Rogers, in a letter to Aberdare, now offered to 'abate' his salary by £120, and, a few days later, announced his intention of resigning at the end of six

[1] Including an attempt to get rid of H. H. Howorth and Major-General A. Stewart Allan from Council. *Cf.* Hyde Clarke to Herbage, 19 Nov., 12, 16 Dec. 1879. R.H.S., H.3/1/1.

[2] *Athenaeum*, 22 Nov. 1879; Scroll Minutes, 15 Jan. 1880.

[3] 17 Jan. 1880 (Rev. R. M. Spence). See also letters in the issue of 3 Jan. 1880.

[4] Rogers to Herbage, 11 March 1880. R.H.S., H.3/1/1; Minutes, 15 July 1880.

[5] Minutes, 26 Jan., 19 Feb., 18 March, 15 April, 17 June 1880.

[6] *Ibid.*, 4 Nov. 1880; Scroll Minutes, 18 Nov. 1880.

months.[1] Finding, however, that he could still count on the support of some members of Council, he began to canvass the formation of a rival society, withdrew his resignation, and issued a printed circular to the Fellows, branding his opponents with 'vile dissimulation' and maligning members of the Committee of Enquiry.[2] This was too much, even for his old adherents. At a special meeting on 5 January 1881 Council demanded his instant resignation, and Rogers wrote it out there and then. But the Report of the Committee of Enquiry, together with a Supplementary Report from the new Council, had still to be laid before the adjourned General Meeting. It met on 12 May. Rogers and his friends were present, 'proceeded in a most disorderly manner', and, when at 10.30 p.m. the Chairman, Cornelius Walford,[3] again adjourned the meeting, went to another room and held a meeting of their own. On the next day Rogers announced that he had again been appointed Secretary and Historiographer, and a notice to this effect appeared in the press, where it was instantly contradicted.[4] Finally, at the further adjourned General Meeting on 19 May, at which 74 persons were present, Aberdare, who had been unable to take the chair a week earlier, himself presided and expressed his entire approval of the Chairman's action at the previous meeting. 'Dr Rogers spoke at some length in his defence', and the Treasurer, now Acting Secretary, replied on behalf of Council. The Supple-

[1] Rogers to Aberdare, 20, 29 Nov. 1880, Minutes, 6 Dec. 1880. The debt, for printing, turned out to be of the order of £250.

[2] Herbage to Zerffi, 23 Dec. 1880, R.H.S., Letter Book, H.3/1/3; Herbage to Clinton, 23 Dec. 1880, *ibid.*; Printed Circular, containing two letters signed by Rogers, 15, 22 Dec. 1880, with postscript dated 30 Dec., and a further circular, also by Rogers, dated 5 May 1881.

[3] 1827–85. A barrister and director of insurance companies, one of Rogers' leading opponents, and the senior Vice-President.

[4] Minutes, 12 May 1881; Rogers to Herbage, 13 May 1881, Agenda Book, 1880–6; *Standard*, 13, 14, 16, 17 May 1881; *Times*, 16, 17 May.

mentary Report was adopted with only three dissentient votes, and a motion that Rogers be re-appointed Secretary was lost by an overwhelming majority, only ten persons voting for it, of whom Rogers himself was one.[1] So ended the second crisis in the history of the Society. The ex-Secretary and Historiographer did his best to discredit still further the Society which had rejected him by publishing yet another pamphlet, *Parting Words to the Members of the Royal Historical Society in a Letter to the President*, by an anonymous article—it could have come from no other pen—entitled 'Cornelius Walford, Projector and Company Monger',[2] and by inspired paragraphs in Scottish and English newspapers accusing the Society, and particularly the Chairman of Council, of ultramontanism, infidelity, atheism and anti-protestantism.[3] His day, however, was done. Returning at last to his native Scotland, he died in Edinburgh in 1890.

It would not have been surprising if the crisis of 1880–1, with all its attendant publicity, had destroyed the Society, or at least damaged it beyond repair. It was not so. On the contrary, with the disappearance of Rogers the decline in membership, begun in 1879, was arrested;[4] financial stability was quickly restored; a capital account was at long last opened in 1882;[5] and new regulations for the Society's government were adopted. They were modelled, Council reported, 'upon those of other learned societies', and they remain, with many modifications, the basis of the present

[1] Minutes, 19 May 1881; *Daily News*, 20 May; *City Press*, 21 May; *Athenaeum*, 28 May.

[2] *Insurance Gazette of Ireland*, iii, No. 10, Oct. 1881.

[3] *Press and St James's Chronicle*, 22 Oct., 3 Sept., 5, 12 Nov. 1881; *Greenock Telegraph*, 11 Oct., 11 Nov. 1881; *Parting Words*.

[4] Ordinary and Life Members: Nov. 1878, 544; Nov. 1879, 520; Jan. 1881, 495; May 1881, 514; Oct. 1881, 536.

[5] *Reports of Council, 1880–1, 1881–2* (17 Nov. 1881, 15 Nov. 1882).

by-laws.[1] The Honorary Treasurer took over the duties of the Secretary until, in 1882, the Society could again afford to employ a paid official; and a Publishing or Publications Committee, thus the oldest of the Society's committees, assumed responsibility for the *Transactions*.[2]

It cannot be said that the *Transactions*, under their new management, showed many or marked signs of improvement, though they did show some: the great change in their character came, not in the 1880's, but in the 1890's. Nor, though a more careful procedure was adopted in the election of Fellows, was any real standard of qualifications imposed. How slender these were is evident from the proposals, from time to time put forward, to send canvassing circulars to the Fellows of the Society of Antiquaries or to the members of the Athenaeum Club.[3] But the gross irregularities of Rogers' day were done away. Council could congratulate the Society in 1887 on 'the sympathy and support' it had gradually enlisted 'of those who are engaged in the cultivation of historical research in London, Oxford and Cambridge';[4] and that this was no idle boast is evident both from the names of new Fellows—Acton, Maitland, Creighton, Lecky, Seeley and Cunningham were all elected between 1884 and 1886—

[1] Minutes, 11 Nov. 1881; *Report of Council, 1880–1*. It was now that the term of office of the President was prescribed as 4 years. But this does not seem to have been thought of as applying to Aberdare.

[2] A new series was begun in 1884, when it was intended to issue them in quarterly parts, which would also contain bibliographical notes and reviews. But the quarterly plan, though long discussed, did not long survive. Nor did the notes and reviews. The place of the Society's *Transactions* as a historical quarterly was taken by the *English Historical Review* in 1886.

[3] A circular was in fact sent to the Fellows of the Society of Antiquaries, drawing their attention to the objects of the Society. *Report of Council, 1888–9*. The question of a canvassing circular continued to be discussed till Oct. 1892, when it was finally dropped.

[4] *Report of Council, 1885–6*.

and from the institution in 1885 of a Cambridge branch, of which Seeley was Chairman and Oscar Browning, now Chairman of Council, Vice-Chairman.[1] It was a sign, also, of better things to come when Council authorised in 1886 and 1889 the preparation of such volumes as Browning's edition of Lord Whitworth's dispatches from Paris in 1803 and Walter of Henley's *Husbandry*.

Four events marked the public progress of the Society: its organisation, in co-operation with the Public Record Office and the British Museum, of the Domesday Commemoration proceedings in 1886; a Conference on Historical Teaching in Schools, the first of its kind, in the following year; and the grant of royal patronage in 1888 and of a royal charter of incorporation in 1889, the year in which the Society came of age.

The work of organising the Domesday Commemoration proceedings, and, later, of editing and publishing the papers then read, fell, for the most part, to a young barrister, Patrick Edward Dove,[2] who had been appointed as the Society's new Secretary, on the recommendation of Lord Aberdare, in March 1882 at a salary of £150 a year. The proceedings themselves were followed, in 1887, by the foundation of the Selden Society, in which Dove shared,[3] and of this society, so dear to Maitland's heart, he became Honorary Secretary and Treasurer, while remaining Secretary of the Royal Historical Society.

The Conference on Historical Teaching in Schools, at which Creighton presided, was reported to have been 'the largest meeting ever got together for the discussion of an

[1] Minutes, 19 March, 21 May 1885. It survived, I think, till Seeley's death in 1895.

[2] 1854–94.

[3] See the preface by Hyde Clarke to vol. i of *Domesday Studies*, ed. P. E. Dove (2 vols., London, 1888, 1891), p. xiv.

educational question',[1] and was a tribute to the energy and enthusiasm of Oscar Browning, who had also been responsible for the establishment of the Cambridge branch of the Society. Four years later—and the hand of Browning is here again evident—Council appointed a committee to consider the development of the study of history in schools. It considered also a proposal that historical societies in the colonies should be affiliated to the Society and that, where they did not exist, the Society should promote or assist their creation.[2] But, like an earlier suggestion that a combination should take place between the Society's *Transactions* and the newly founded *English Historical Review*,[3] and, like proposals to establish secretaries and to hold lectures outside London,[4] these projects died at birth—except for the foundation of the Cambridge branch. It was to be left for the Historical Association to do what the Royal Historical Society failed to do.

For the royal patronage and the royal charter[5] the Society was indebted to Lord Aberdare. Aberdare was the son-in-law and biographer of Sir William Napier, the historian of the Peninsular War, and, as such, in Tout's words, had 'a quasi-hereditary title to be considered as a military historian'. As Tout also observed, he was the first President to take his office seriously, frequently attending, unlike his predecessors, the meetings of Council, but, like Russell, delivering

---

[1] *Report of Council, 1886–7.* Browning's address is printed in *Transactions*, n.s., iv (1889), pp. 69–81.

[2] Minutes, 20 March, 15 May, 19 June 1890.

[3] *Ibid.*, 20 Jan. 1887.

[4] *Ibid.*, 9 Nov. 1876 (establishment of local secretaries); 19 March, 21 May 1885 (establishment of Cambridge branch); 4 Nov. 1880: 'The Council engaged that Lectures in History should be delivered in the principal towns'.

[5] The draft was drawn up by Dove. Letters Patent were issued on 31 July 1889.

only one presidential address. He expressed a wish to retire in February 1890, and Council, through Oscar Browning, offered the presidency first to S. R. Gardiner, then to Lord Rosebery, and finally to Sir Mountstuart Elphinstone Grant Duff,[1] who—to quote Tout again—'was a more literary variant of the type of his predecessor' and, 'as the son of the historian of the Mahrattas', had 'a stronger claim to be a hereditary historian than the son-in-law of the historian of the Peninsular War'.[2]

Grant Duff set the precedent, in his two terms, of delivering annual presidential addresses. These are of the kind that the reader of the many volumes of his *Notes from a Diary* might expect: elegant allocutions, usually on classical themes, which contrast strangely with the papers that were now appearing in *Transactions*. But he was a loyal and hard-working President and so regular in attendance at Council's meetings that the office of Chairman became redundant and was abolished in 1894.

More important than the transition from Aberdare to Grant Duff was a further administrative re-organisation of the Society: the revision of its by-laws in 1889; the appointment of a Finance Committee in 1890 and of a Library Committee in 1891;[3] and the institution, again at the instance of Oscar Browning, of a Director, who, as a 'professional historian', was to be responsible for the Society's publications and for the papers read. This innovation, or reversion, as it really was, to the office of Historiographer, was carried through only in the face of strong opposition, some of it, one may suspect, on the part of the Secretary. The decision to institute the office of Director was approved

---

[1] 1829–1906. Under-Secretary of State for India, 1868–74, and for Colonies, 1880; Governor of Madras, 1881–6; F.R.S., 1901.

[2] Tout, *op. cit.*, pp. 9, 15.

[3] Minutes, 19 Jan., 20 Feb. 1890, 18 June, 17 Dec. 1891.

by one vote only; so too was the decision to proceed to an appointment one month later, on 19 March 1891. And it was only by the casting vote of the President that Hubert Hall, at this time a clerk in the Public Record Office, was then appointed Director, with a stipend of £50 a year.[1] Appointed for two years, he remained Director for forty-seven.

While the Director's duties were now defined, so also were the composition, duties and procedures of the Finance, Publications and Library Committees.[2] The first of these instituted successive purges of those Fellows who were in arrears of subscriptions. The second put forward a plan, for which Hall and Browning seem primarily to have been responsible, for the initiation of a continuing and uniform series of volumes of original source materials.[3] The third superintended the removal of the library to a room in St Martin's Free Library, St Martin's Lane. The library had been in store since 1884. Now the postal wrappers on hundreds of parts of the proceedings of other societies were for the first time removed, the postmarks on the unopened parcels extending over a period of seven years.[4] A librarian[5] was appointed and the books and pamphlets were catalogued. All in all the Society might well have congratulated itself, in the early 1890's, on a new era opening before it.

Its troubles, however, were not yet over. In May 1894 Council resolved to take steps to commemorate the centenary of the death of Gibbon. An impressive committee was appointed, containing such names as those of Mommsen, Harnack, Lavisse and Gross from overseas, and of Acton, Maitland, Bryce and Dicey at home. Dove and Hall were

---

[1] Minutes, 20 Nov., 18 Dec. 1890, 19 Feb., 19 March 1891.
[2] *Ibid.*, 17 March 1892.
[3] *Ibid.*, 16 Feb. 1893.
[4] *Ibid.*, 19 May 1892.
[5] Thomas Mason, the Librarian at St Martin's Public Library.

appointed joint-secretaries. Exhibitions and lectures were arranged at the British Museum, and the celebrations began on 15 November. Six days later Dove destroyed himself. The shock to the Society and to the Selden Society, of which Dove was Treasurer as well as Honorary Secretary, was the greater when it became almost immediately apparent that monies belonging to both societies had disappeared. The chief loss fell upon the Selden Society, which Maitland at first feared must be brought to as honourable an end as possible. The Royal Historical Society suffered less financial embarrassment, though it had to make good subscriptions paid on behalf of the Gibbon Commemoration; it was involved in difficulties with its printers, who were also the printers to the Selden Society; and it was unable to recover some of the books and papers which had been in Dove's possession.[1]

As with the Selden Society, however, so with the Royal Historical Society, the loyalty of the members survived the defalcations of the Secretary, of which, indeed, very little was known to the world at large. The Director himself took over the secretaryship for the next few years, the Librarian assuming also the duties of a clerk.[2] Plans were announced for further documentary publications. And though, in the 1890's, the membership was again falling—due partly to the removal of defaulters and partly also, no doubt, to a more

---

[1] Maitland to J. B. Thayer, 25 Nov. 1894. C. H. S. Fifoot, *The Letters of Frederic William Maitland* (Selden Society, 1965), pp. 141–2. Dove was indebted to the Selden Society for roughly £1,000, to the Royal Historical Society for £74. Selden Society, Minutes, 8 March 1895; *Proceedings of the Gibbon Commemoration, 1794–1894* (London, 1895), Report of the Honorary Secretary, p. 8; *Report on the State of the Society's Foreign Exchanges*, 10 Dec. 1898; Hall to Tout, 2 Feb. 1926, Tout Papers.

[2] The salary of the Director was fixed at £126, that of the Librarian and Clerk at £30.

discriminating election policy and to the more scholarly nature of the Society's activities—the prospects for the future were greatly enhanced when, early in 1896, the Camden Society, one of the most important of English publishing societies, approached the Royal Historical Society with a proposal for amalgamation. The proposal was approved at a special meeting on 19 November and the amalgamation came into effect on 1 May 1897. The members of the Camden Society became Fellows of the Royal Historical Society—a welcome accession—three of them with a seat on Council. The Royal Historical Society took over the balance of the Camden Society's funds[1] and its other assets. And it was agreed that the great series of Camden volumes, of which more than 160 had appeared, should be continued as the publications of the Royal Historical Society. Hubert Hall may have been right when he wrote, many years later, that the Camden Society 'collapsed simply from boredom. The leaders were bored by the Society and the Society was bored by the leaders' insistence on Stuart and Tudor topics'.[2] But whether Hall was right or wrong, the amalgamation, in which he played a major part, was a watershed in the Society's history. The age of the dilettanti had ended.

The signs of the professionalisation of the Society had been increasingly marked in the 1890's. The appointment of Hall as Director in 1891, the changing character of *Transactions*, the new programme of scholarly research, the election of such men as Vinogradoff, John Franklin Jameson and Charles Gross as Corresponding Fellows and of Mommsen as an Honorary Fellow, all pointed the same way. For the first time serious attention had been given to the library and to library policy, and libraries themselves, in increasing

---

[1] The sum of £225 4s. 4d. was paid over, and 84 members of the Camden Society were elected Fellows.

[2] Hall to Tout, 2 Feb. 1926, Tout Papers.

numbers, began to apply for membership.[1] Frederic Harrison pleaded before the Society for 'a scientific bibliography of the published materials' for English history, and York Powell for the training of archivists and the establishment of local record offices.[2] In 1897 Louis Charles Alexander, the Society's first Secretary, who had resumed his membership on the retirement of Rogers, endowed the Society with the Alexander Medal,[3] and the first of a long and notable series of Alexander Prize Essays was presented in 1898. And in 1899, at the end of Grant Duff's second term, a decisive change occurred in the character of the presidency. It was the change from the man of letters or man of affairs to the working historian. 'We want a *strong* man and a scholar', wrote Hall.[4] And the Society was fortunate in the result. Sir Edward Maunde Thompson, of the British Museum, Prothero, who had recently announced his resignation from the Chair of History at Edinburgh in order to edit the *Quarterly Review*, Lord Edmond Fitzmaurice, were each approached in turn. Then, in April 1899, A. W. Ward was nominated. Less than two years later, when ill-health and his election to the Mastership of Peterhouse dictated Ward's resignation,[5]

[1] Libraries had been admitted from the early days. But not many joined before 1897, the date of the amalgamation with the Camden Society. In order to place future subscribing libraries on an equal footing with those already admitted as members of the Camden Society, Council resolved that libraries should pay the amount that the Camden Society had charged, namely £1 p.a. By 1901 the number of subscribing libraries had reached 130.

[2] *Transactions*, n.s., xi (1897), pp. 19–30, 31–40.

[3] He proposed a gold medal, but the Society had to be content with silver. The benefaction took the form of a Russian 4% Railway Bond, 1889, valued at £98 17s. 6d., which became worthless in 1918. The prize essay was established in 1898 after Council had failed to induce S. R. Gardiner to be the Alexander Medallist.

[4] Hall to Tout, 21 Jan. 1899, Tout Papers.

[5] Minutes, 17 Jan. 1901; Ward to Tout, 5 Feb. 1901, Tout Papers.

c

Prothero was again offered the presidency and this time accepted it. So, in turn, two of the men who had done most to secure a re-organisation of historical studies during the last thirty years each became President of the Society.

Whatever the progress made in these years so far as under-graduate teaching was concerned, when Ward took office not only was there no such thing as a 'History School' in London itself, there was 'no real school of research in History in any English University'. These were the words of A. F. Pollard,[1] who was appointed to a part-time Chair of Constitutional History at University College London in 1903. And Prothero, two years earlier, had said much the same thing. 'There was plenty of historical teaching', he wrote, 'but little training in method; plenty of instruction in reading but little in the art of writing history; next to none in the science of drawing historical conclusions from original documents, whether manuscript or printed.'[2]

This was the deficiency which Ward and Prothero, with the full support of Council, sought to remedy. They emphasised, as Pollard was also to emphasise, in very similar language, the neglected opportunities and unequalled resources awaiting the research student in London. They pointed, as York Powell had pointed, to the example of the École des Chartes at Paris and to the practice of the continental universities and of the Johns Hopkins University in the United States; and they proposed the establishment of a School of Advanced Historical Studies in London, ultimately to become, like the recently established School of Economics, a School of the University, which would provide

---

[1] 'The University of London and the Study of History' [Oct. 1904], in A. F. Pollard, *Factors in Modern History* (London, 1907), pp. 262–287.

[2] Presidential Address, 20 Feb. 1902. *Transactions*, n.s., xvi (1902), p. xix.

courses on the nature and treatment of historical sources, printed and unprinted, and on bibliography, methodology, palaeography and diplomatic; would arrange for instruction in other auxiliary sciences and in special subjects; and would provide, by means of the seminar method, the criticism and guidance which advanced students needed. It was Ward's view that such a School would not only be of immense value at home but that 'American and other foreign students' would gladly avail themselves of its facilities while working in England.[1]

The outlines of this plan were discussed by Ward with members of the Society in 1899, laid before Council in January 1900 and reported on by a committee which included both Prothero and Hall. A circular letter signed by Ward as President and thirty-five members of Council was then sent to some three hundred distinguished persons and students of history. A large and influential general committee was established,[2] and at a meeting in December, at which James Bryce took the chair, an Executive Committee was set up with Bryce as Chairman and Hall as Secretary. On this same day the Bishop of London died, and a movement was at once set on foot to establish a memorial to him. It was hoped that the foundation of a Chair of History in London would form a part of this, and the new Committee for Advanced Historical Teaching prepared, therefore, to join forces with

[1] *Ibid.*, n.s., xiv (1900), pp. 15–18 (Ward), xvi (1902), pp. xviii–xxii (Prothero); Typescript by Hall, 'Advanced Historical Studies in London' [n.d., 1901], and memorandum dated 25 Feb. 1901, R.H.S., Prothero Papers, 2/iii/4; Printed Circulars, headed Royal Historical Society [8 Oct.] and 30 Nov. 1900. See also the *Reports* of the Committee of Management of the Advanced Historical Teaching Fund.

[2] The first circular [8 Oct.] was signed not only by Ward and Prothero but by Acton, Firth, Gardiner, Gasquet, Lecky, Maitland, Ramsay, Oman and Tout. The General Committee comprised over 160 persons, including distinguished foreigners.

the Creighton Memorial Committee. But in vain. The requisite funds could not be found to endow in the capital city of the empire a chair in memory of its bishop, and all that resulted from the two movements was the establishment of an annual Creighton Lecture in the University of London and the temporary provision of two lectureships, each worth £100 a year, at the London School of Economics. Not till after the First World War was the plan, devised by Ward and promulgated by the Society, revived and carried to triumphant success by Pollard, with the foundation in 1921 of the Institute of Historical Research.

Neither Ward nor Prothero, nor the Society as such, was directly concerned with the inception of a second great enterprise in 1906, the foundation of the Historical Association. The School of Advanced Historical Studies was intended to be a post-graduate school. The Historical Association was thought of at first as a body whose primary aim lay in 'the advancement and co-ordination of historical teaching in schools', though some of its founders had a wider purpose.[1] Council welcomed it. Many of the Fellows of the Society warmly supported it.[2] And while, in 1905, the Society had dreamt, for a moment, of itself housing the School of Advanced Historical Studies,[3] provided the Government or some 'munificent benefactor' would put rooms at its disposal, in 1906, and for thirty years, it did house the offices of the Historical Association, not only without charge in the

[1] *Report of Council, 1905–6; The Historical Association, 1906–1956* (London, 1955), pp. 7–9.
[2] Ward and Prothero were both Vice-Presidents; and Firth, the President of the Historical Association, was a Vice-President of the Society.
[3] *Report of Council, 1904–5.* The School was represented by the two lecturers, of whom Hall was one. But it was still hoped to secure a much wider extension of the work and the creation of a real 'post-graduate' school. *Transactions*, n.s., xix (1905), pp. 12–13.

earlier days, but allowing also its paid Assistant Secretary to become the Secretary of the Association.

The Society welcomed the Association as a 'valuable adjunct' to its own work[1] but in a sphere which it did not itself think of penetrating. Prothero in 1904, like Firth, who became Regius Professor of Modern History at Oxford in this same year, and like Pollard in London, had vigorously criticised the neglect of nineteenth-century, or recent, history in British universities;[2] and no doubt it was as a result of this, and of his later recommendation that the Society's *Transactions* should not be 'too exclusively insular and medieval', that Council announced its intention to give preference to papers dealing with the modern period and with general historical subjects.[3] But the Society did not itself take up the question of the teaching of history, apart from 'advanced history', in universities and schools. As in an earlier day, local secretaries were again appointed, at Oxford, Cambridge, Manchester and elsewhere, 'recruiting sergeants', Prothero called them, in the persons of Firth, J. R. Tanner and Tout, 'to beat up young and active soldiers for our ranks'; for these, he held, with Council, should include '*all* historians' who had 'made any mark in historical science'.[4] But the Society did not contemplate, as it once had contemplated, the establishment of local branches, such as the

---

[1] *Reports of Council, 1905–6, 1908–9.*

[2] Presidential Address, 18 Feb. 1904. *Transactions*, n.s., xviii (1904), pp. 12–31. Firth, writing to Prothero on 22 Jan. 1904, denounced the 'imbecile conservatism' at Oxford by which 'the neglect of recent history becomes more accentuated every year'. R.H.S., Prothero Papers, 2/iii/4.

[3] Presidential Address, 16 Feb. 1905, *Transactions*, n.s., xix (1905), pp. 15–17; *Report of Council, 1904–5.*

[4] Minutes, 17 Nov., 15 Dec. 1904; 16 March 1905 (A. Grant, Leeds); 20 June 1907 (R. S. Lepper, India); *Transactions*, n.s., xix (1905), p. 5; xviii (1904), p. 3.

Historical Association was to establish, or the holding of lectures outside London.

Ward had taken the view that 'the first title' of the Society to 'confidence and support' lay in its 'work as a publishing society';[1] and this, to a very considerable extent, was Prothero's view too. It is an indication of fundamental purpose, as well as of current costs and relative prosperity, that he could declare, in 1905: 'with strict economy and careful management, we shall be able to devote £400 yearly (that is, nearly two-thirds of our income) to our primary object— the publication of a volume of Transactions and two volumes of Camden books every year'. But if this was the primary object, it was not the only one. 'We exist', he said, 'primarily for the making and publication of books . . . That is true enough; this is the limit of our present aims and utility. But', he went on, 'I desire to see this Society something more than a publishing society. I desire to see it placed in a better position for the promotion and encouragement of historical study. Its rooms should be a centre where all historians, British and foreign, may meet—an armoury where all persons engaged in historical research may find the weapons necessary for starting and carrying on their work.'[2]

One weapon in the armoury he disclosed in a letter to Tout in 1902. 'I have a big project in my mind just now', he wrote, '—that of an historical bibliography for Great Britain and Ireland, since the Middle Ages, to be carried through by co-operation on a large scale by members of the Hist. Soc?.'[3] Such a project had been discussed by H. R. Tedder,[4] the Secretary and Librarian of the Athenaeum, in 1885 and again by Frederic Harrison in 1896. For Prothero

[1] *Transactions*, n.s., xiv (1900), p. 7.
[2] *Ibid.*, n.s., xix (1905), pp. 4, 11.
[3] 10 Nov. 1902, Tout Papers.
[4] Hon. Treasurer, 1904–24.

it was to be a continuation of the great work of Charles Gross,[1] and in his presidential address in 1903 he gave it definite shape and form.[2] Not, however, till after his retirement was the scheme carried further. The American Historical Association took up a parallel project in 1908. At Firth's suggestion the Society and the Association agreed to co-operate, and in 1909 a Joint Committee of the two bodies was established, a plan for the bibliography was approved, and Prothero himself was appointed general editor.[3]

The production of a *Bibliography of British History*, the removal of what he described as 'both a reproach and a hindrance to British historical scholarship', was one weapon in Prothero's armoury. But an armoury meant a library—a working library, that is, containing the tools of the historian's trade. His own library has been described as 'the library of an Institute of Historical Research in embryo',[4] and this is what he wanted the Society's library to be.[5] It was very far from that. But both during his presidency and afterwards it was constantly enriched by his gifts, and ultimately it inherited his own fine collection. For the first time, moreover, in June 1901, it obtained a home of its own, when the Society took a lease of 3 Serjeants' Inn, Chancery Lane.[6]

[1] *Sources and Literature of English History from the earliest times to about 1485* (London and New York, 1900).

[2] *Transactions*, n.s., xvii (1903), pp. ix–xxxiv.

[3] American Historical Association, *Annual Report*, 1908 (Washington, 1909), i, p. 93; Minutes, 18 March 1909, 15 Dec. 1910; H. R. Tedder, in *Transactions*, 3rd ser., viii (1914), pp. 41–54.

[4] Typescript by H. H. Bellot, 9 Nov. 1967.

[5] *Transactions*, n.s., xix (1905), pp. 8–12.

[6] The Library had been moved to the St Martin's Free Library, 115 St Martin's Lane, in 1892 and a small room there had been set aside also for the meetings of Council. Council began to meet there in 1893. But the general meetings continued to be held at Hanover Square till November 1894, when they were transferred to the Museum of Practical Geology, Jermyn Street. Council sometimes met there

Much miscellaneous material, 'in a filthy and verminous condition', hitherto stored in a basement room, was discarded, and efforts were made to fill the gaps in what was described as the Society's unique series of foreign *Transactions* as well as to remedy other deficiencies.[1] But the rooms in Serjeants' Inn barely survived Prothero's presidency. The Inn was destined for demolition, and the Society, rejecting a proposal by Pollard that it should move its library and offices to University College[2] (where they now are), took refuge at 7 South Square, Gray's Inn.

'25 Feb. Hist. Soc. C[ttee]. revised rules—passed all my proposed amendments which I had drafted', reads an entry in Prothero's diary in 1902. The amendments related for the most part to the institution of a class of Honorary Vice-Presidents,[3] who would be relieved of the duty of attending Council, to the number of ordinary Vice-Presidents and Councillors, and to the admission of subscribing libraries. A year later the duties of the Director (now, for the first time, styled Literary Director) and of an Honorary Secretary were again divided and defined.[4] Hubert Hall remained in the former office with a salary of a hundred guineas. H. E. Malden, who, as a former Scholar of Trinity Hall and a lecturer for the Cambridge University Extension scheme,

---

also. The room in St Martin's Lane was retained till March 1901. The Council met in its own first home in June 1901. The general meetings thereafter were held in the Old Hall of Clifford's Inn. The rent of Serjeants' Inn was £80 p.a.

[1] Library Committee Minutes, 27 June 1901; Director's Report on Exchanges, 18 March 1903, Minutes, 22 Oct. 1903. For the foreign publications in the Library see *Transactions*, n.s., xviii (1904), pp. 380–91.

[2] Minutes, 21 June 1906.

[3] But past Presidents became Hon. Vice-Presidents under the Rules drawn up in 1881.

[4] Minutes, 21 May 1903.

had been recommended for the post of paid Secretary on Rogers' retirement in 1881,[1] now became, twenty-two years later, Honorary Secretary instead, so to remain for nearly twenty-eight years more. The opportunity was also taken to elevate the office of clerk, now held by Miss M. B. Curran,[2] formerly of Girton, to that of Assistant Secretary, and Miss Curran was to remain Assistant Secretary, not for twenty-eight years, but for forty, combining with this post, for fifteen, that of Secretary of the Historical Association.

Prothero has rightly been called 'almost a second founder' of the Society.[3] It inherited, in 1934, the bulk of his estate— a bequest amounting to over £22,400, in addition to his library; and it is fitting that in the centenary year an annual lectureship should have been instituted in his memory. He left the Society in 1905 steadily advancing in reputation, its finances in good order, and its membership, if not as extensive as he wished it to be, on the way to becoming, in kind, what he hoped: 'in some degree a distinction, or at least a mark of genuine interest in, and some knowledge of, historical science'.[4] The subscribing libraries at home and abroad already numbered more than 150 and among the Fellows could be counted a fair sprinkling overseas, in the United States, Canada, India, Australia and South Africa.

For the next fifteen years the Society pursued the 'modest and even tenor' of its way, without much internal incident until the eve of the First World War. William Hunt, William Cunningham, Charles Firth and Charles Oman in turn

[1] Aberdare to Zerffi, 14 Feb. 1881. R.H.S., H.3/1/1.

[2] Miss Curran had been appointed librarian and clerk (part-time) at a salary of £50 p.a. in May 1901.

[3] *Report of Council, 1921–22; Transactions*, 4th ser., vi (1923), pp. 171–2.

[4] *Transactions*, n.s., xix (1905), p. 5. The Society's income had risen from under £500 in 1896 to more than £800 in 1904, and its reserves, in this latter year, amounted to over £1,000.

occupied the presidency, Firth and Oman during the pre-
occupations of the war years. The Society and its officers
played a leading part in the International Historical Congress
held in London in 1913.[1] Its publications appeared with ad-
mirable regularity,[2] and its plans for the *Bibliography of
British History* were so far advanced that an appeal for subscriptions could be issued in June 1912, the Society itself, the
American Historical Association and the British Academy
all having promised modest subventions.[3] But the outbreak
of the war called a halt to the *Bibliography*, as it put a stop,
also, to the preparations which were being made for the celebration of the 700th anniversary of Magna Carta.[4] In need of
larger premises, the Society had already arranged, before the
war began, to take over, on a long lease, a large house at
22 Russell Square.[5] There it removed in December, 1914, to
become host to a number of other societies,[6] providing the
American Historical Association with its short-lived London
headquarters from 1914 to 1920,[7] housing the Historical
Association, and running, during the war years, a series of
evening lectures on subjects of general and topical interest,

[1] *Report of Council, 1912–13; Transactions*, 4th ser., ix (1926), p. 24.

[2] There were only two years, 1918 and 1921, in which no Camden
volume appeared. But while two volumes were published in each year
from 1908 to 1912, only one volume a year was published from 1913
to 1917.

[3] Minutes, 15 Dec. 1910, 19 Jan. 1911; *Reports of Council, 1909–10,
1910–11*.

[4] But a volume of *Magna Carta Commemoration Essays* was published in 1917.

[5] At a rental of £170 p.a.

[6] Including, at one time or another, the British Archaeological
Association, the Japan Society, the Royal Numismatic Society and the
Huguenot Society.

[7] See E. Donnan and L. F. Stock, eds., *An Historian's World. Selec-
tions from the Correspondence of John Franklin Jameson* (Philadelphia,
1956), pp. 164–5.

on historical documents and records, on the 'Map of Europe by Treaty', and on imperial and colonial history.

Tout, looking back in 1926, as the second of the post-war Presidents (he succeeded J. W. Fortescue and was himself succeeded by Sir Richard Lodge), spoke of the 'four years of stagnation' during the war and of 'six of slowly winning back our lost ground'.[1] But it may be questioned how much of the ground was in fact made good. The Society, it is true, took its public duties seriously, constituting in 1918, for example, a Records Committee on which all members of the former Royal Commission on Public Records served, and which was designed to hasten the publication of the Commission's Third Report and the implementation of its recommendations.[2] In 1921 when its part-time Assistant Secretary became full-time[3] and so ceased to be the Secretary of the Historical Association, it wisely sought means of closer co-operation with that body.[4] On the death of Prothero in 1922, it set up a consultative committee to carry on his work, in conjunction with the American Historical Association, though on a slightly altered plan, for the *Bibliography of British History*. As a result, the seventeenth-century volume, edited by one of Firth's former pupils,

[1] *Transactions*, 4th ser., ix (1926), p. 25.

[2] Minutes, 11 April 1918, 13 March 1919, *Reports of Council, 1917–1918, 1918–19, 1919–20*; Minutes of Records Committee; and see Hubert Hall, *A Repertory of British Archives: Part I, England*, published by the Society in 1920, pp. xxxiv–xliii. Hall had been secretary of the Commission. Council wrote to the Home Secretary and to the Master of the Rolls and sent a memorial to the Treasury.

[3] At a salary of £300 p.a. Minutes, 10 Feb. 1921, 12 May 1921.

[4] Minutes, 9 Dec. 1920, 10 March 1921. Members of the Historical Association were permitted to read in the Society's library and there was to be more co-operation between the two Societies 'in the way of facilities' for attending each other's meetings. For two or three years a joint meeting was held between representatives of the Society and of the Association.

Godfrey Davies, was published by the Clarendon Press in 1928, and the sixteenth-century volume, which Conyers Read edited in the United States, appeared five years later.[1] An editor was also, at long last, found for an eighteenth-century volume.[2] All this was on the credit side. And the Society might congratulate itself also, as Tout congratulated it in 1929[3]—a year in which it was endowed with a second prize essay, this time in Scottish history[4]—on the increasing support it drew from subscribing libraries and among Fellows overseas.

But there was a debit side too. Council was persuaded in 1921 to institute what it called a sub-series of the Camden Series intended to illustrate the character and continuity of British foreign policy. The proposal came from A. F. Basil Williams, who wished to see a series of volumes containing the instructions given to British ambassadors and diplomatic agents between 1689 and 1789, parallel to the *Recueil des Instructions données aux Ambassadeurs de France* published by the Commission des Archives Diplomatiques. The analogy, as Council was well aware, was not a true one. Hall himself pointed out that the French instructions were in fact *mémoires* which 'supplied a general view of the political situation'; the British instructions were not, and needed, therefore, to be supplemented by other documents. But Hall and the Council allowed themselves to be convinced,[5] and,

[1] Minutes, Bibliography Cttee., 21 Dec. 1922, 14 Feb. 1923, 10 May 1923; *Reports of Council*, *1922–3*, *1925–6*. An American Committee took charge of the Tudor volume, a British of the Stuart.

[2] D. J. Medley, who had recently retired from his Chair at the University of Glasgow. Minutes, 9 Feb. 1933.

[3] *Transactions*, 4th ser., xii (1929), p. 2.

[4] Created by the will of David Anderson Berry, in memory of his father, the Rev. David Berry.

[5] Minutes, 11 March 1920, 10 June 1920, 14 April 1921; *Reports of*

beginning in 1922, the Society issued a series of *British Diplomatic Instructions*, for Sweden, France and Denmark, which, however ably edited, were no more than a mere selection from dispatches, and of which seven volumes were published, at considerable expense, before a later Council succeeded in bringing the series to a close.[1] Of the series of *Diplomatic Instructions* H. W. V. Temperley went so far as to say that they hazarded 'the reputation of British historical scholarship'.[2] Certainly they did nothing to enhance that of the Society, which may well have been damaged also—and deservedly so—by an indiscriminate invitation to all history professors and delegates attending the first Anglo-American Historical Conference in 1921 to apply for the Fellowship of the Society if they were not Fellows already.[3] But there were other grounds for disquiet. Just as the Historical Association had taken for its own the educational work which the Society had not wanted to do, and was rapidly expanding in the post-war years, so, in 1921, the opening of the Institute of Historical Research, that School of Advanced Historical Studies which the Society had formerly advocated, and which was far more richly endowed than the Society itself, 'swept whole fields of historical activity' out of its grasp.[4] As for the Society's library, far from becoming the working library which Prothero had envisaged, it had degenerated into a large but miscellaneous assembly of books covering all sorts of historical fields and periods,

Council, 1919-20, 1920-1; Report by Hall on the Publication of Diplomatic Instructions [1920]. R.H.S., H.4/1.

[1] The two volumes of *British Diplomatic Representatives*, published in 1932 and 1934, formed no part of this series. These were issued at the recommendation of H. W. V. Temperley in the first instance and then of C. K. Webster. Minutes, 8 Dec. 1927, 18 April 1928.

[2] *English Historical Review*, xxxviii (1923), pp. 281–3.

[3] Minutes, 7 July 1921.

[4] H. H. Bellot, *op. cit.*

to which had been added, despite Prothero's warnings,[1] a still more miscellaneous collection of manuscripts.

It is impossible not to feel that the Society, in the 1920's, though the official representative of British historical scholarship at home and abroad, had lost its sense of purpose, was increasingly out of touch with the currents of research in the universities, and had entered into a period of lethargy which inevitably meant decline. To Hall, who had been Director since 1891, the Society owed an enormous debt. Maitland said of him that he was 'the most unselfish man' he had ever known, Jameson that he had been 'the friend of all American students at the Public Record Office', from which he retired in 1921.[2] He had devotion, energy and self-denial.[3] But the brief introduction to his *List and Index* of the Society's publications which he produced in 1925 abounds in errors; well might it have been said of him that 'literary men are seldom . . . good men of business'; and his own contacts with the academic world, in the 1920's, were with the older, not the younger, scholars, and had grown increasingly tenuous.

'And now what about our Society, with its house, its library, its considerable funds?', asked F. M. Powicke, who had been called to the Regius Chair of Modern History at Oxford in 1928, in a paper on 'Modern Methods of Medieval Research', which he read to the Society on 8 December 1932.[4] 'We are naturally expected', he said, 'to take a leading

[1] *Transactions*, n.s., xix (1905), p. 12.

[2] Maitland to R. L. Poole, 7 Sept. 1898. Fifoot, *Letters of F. W. Maitland*, pp. 224–5; Jameson to Bryce, 7 Jan. 1914, *An Historian's World*, p. 164. But Maitland added, 'Poor Hall has a curious fluffy mind'.

[3] R. L. Poole (who had a low opinion, however, of Hall as a scholar) to Prothero, 26 June 1902, Prothero Papers, 2/iii/4.

[4] *Transactions*, 4th ser., xvi (1933), pp. 45–53. Reprinted in *Modern Historians and the Study of History: Essays and Papers* (London, 1955), pp. 193–9.

place in the historical world . . . But ought the Society to have a deliberate, permanent policy . . .? Would it be possible . . . to make our library, not only a centre, but *the* centre and home of local record publications . . .? As we are inclined to raise the qualifications required for election as a fellow of the Society, could we strengthen our position and enlarge our membership by erecting a class of Associates . . .?' And, he added, 'how can we best relate our normal traditional activities, particularly as publishers, to the learned world about us?'.

No such questions had been asked since Prothero's day, and they gained an added significance because on this same 8 December, at the first contested nomination in the Society's history, Powicke was proposed for the presidency. It is some indication of the feeling in the Society that in November fourteen Vice-Presidents and members of Council and four other Fellows had sent a letter to Lodge, as President, nominating Powicke for election at the Anniversary Meeting in February, 1933. The action was wholly unprecedented and in Lodge's view unconstitutional. But at the December Council the innovators had their way, though two other names were put forward; and in February Powicke was elected.[1]

Now began a renovation of the Society's activities. A sub-committee of the Publications Committee in 1933 recommended the establishment of a new series of publications, in addition to the Camden Series, to include such types of material as guides, handbooks and aids to historical research in general, and to serve in particular the interests of students of modern history.[2] A 'Committee on Future Needs' proposed a revision of the Society's administrative machinery,

[1] Minutes, 10 Nov., 8 Dec. 1932; Address to Lodge, 8 Nov. 1932. R.H.S., H.3/2/3/3.
[2] Minutes, 9 March, 28 Sept. 1933.

more particularly of the structure of its committees, in order
to secure the more efficient conduct of business; the introduction of a pension scheme for full-time officers; the reconstruction of the library; and the establishment of a new
class of Associate Members, to link to the Society, it was
suggested, 'the members of local record and historical societies and younger graduates engaged in historical research'.[1]
In September—it is the symbol of a new day—the minutes
of Council, hitherto written in long-hand,[2] were for the first
time typed and circulated, together with other papers. And
in January 1934 Council invited H. Hale Bellot to accept the
Honorary Secretaryship. This had been only temporarily
filled since the death of H. E. Malden, at the age of 82, in
1931. 'As you know', wrote Powicke, in words which are an
interesting commentary on contemporary conditions, 'there
is very little work . . . But the position of Secretary is very
important in giving the holder influence'.[3] No doubt it was.
But if the influence already existed, so, soon, did the work.
And the Society can only be grateful that Professor Bellot
should have exercised the one while performing the other
for more than eighteen years, until his long and distinguished
service as Secretary terminated with his election to the presidency in 1952.[4]

Almost the whole of the programme outlined in 1932 was
put into effect in the next few years. The first volume in the
Guides and Handbooks Series, Sir George Clark's *Guide to
English commercial statistics, 1696–1782,* was published in
1938, and the second, the *Handbook of British chronology,*

[1] Report of the Committee of Council on Future Needs, [9 Nov.
1933]; Minutes, 9 Nov. 1933.

[2] The Minutes, however, continued to be entered into the Minute
Book in long-hand till 11 Feb. 1937.

[3] Powicke to Bellot, 16 Jan. 1934. Bellot Papers.

[4] He served the Society once again as Acting-Secretary during the
illness of the Secretary from May 1960 to March 1961.

which Powicke himself edited and which was an example of
the kind of co-operative work he wished the Society to
undertake, appeared in the following year. By this time it
had become clear that the new series, which some members
of Council had criticized on the ground that the Society
should concern itself, not with guides or bibliographies, but
only with the preparation of texts, was proving to be quite
as valuable to the medievalist as to the modernist. Meanwhile, a number of administrative reforms had been sanc-
tioned in February 1934, the class of Associate Members
created in May,[1] and plans for the reconstruction of the
library approved in October. The library, greatly enriched
by the incorporation, after the death of Lady Prothero in
April, of the most significant part of Sir George Prothero's
own library, was at long last given a precise function both
as a lending and as a reference library. It was re-designed so
as to provide with some degree of completeness the aids to
research, the texts, and the works of reference which a research institution ought properly to supply for the student
of British history, and no longer to attempt the impossible
task, in a more sophisticated library world, of catering for all
historical periods and subjects.[2]

[1] The Associate class was meant to exclude persons 'in statu
pupillari' but to include graduate students working under supervision,
as well as persons who, as investigators, administrators or teachers,
were actively engaged in historical work but were not fully qualified
for election to the Fellowship.

[2] Report of the Library Committee, Minutes, 11 Oct. 1934. The
library was at first meant to provide for colonial as well as British
history. But this proved to be too ambitious an enterprise. Minutes,
10 Nov. 1938. *Texts and Calendars: an analytical guide to serial publications*, by E. L. C. Mullins (1958), provided a guide to one of the most
important sections of the library. A number of special collections
within the Library have been donated by the Society to more appro-
priate custodians: the Robinson Genealogical MSS. to the Society of

D

Not content with these achievements, the President put forward what he called 'a pet scheme of mine for a new edition of Gross',[1] and the Honorary Secretary a plan for an annual list of writings on British history, comparable with the great series of *Writings on American History* and similar lists for France and Germany.[2] Of these proposals the first was taken in hand by the Medieval Academy of America with the Society's support and co-operation.[3] The second was made practicable by the new source of income accruing to the Society as the residuary legatee of Sir George Prothero's estate.[4] A compiler and editor was found in the person of A. T. Milne, who was appointed Assistant Officer in 1935, and the first volume of *Writings on British History* was published in 1937.

Finally, in 1937, the Society again moved its home. The lease of its house in Russell Square was due to expire in 1939. It could only be renewed at a much higher rent, resulting in

Genealogists, the Hensman collections relating to the Civil War in the Midlands to the Northamptonshire Record Society, the Lloyd Collection on Military History to King's College, London, and various miscellaneous manuscript and pamphlet collections to the British Museum and the Public Record Office.

[1] Powicke to Bellot, 8 Feb. 1935, Bellot Papers; Minutes, 14 March, 10 Oct. 1935.

[2] Proposal for the Publication of an Annual Bibliography of English History [1935]; Minutes, 14 March 1935; 11 June 1936.

[3] The Society was represented upon an advisory board and contributed £300 to the cost of preparing the manuscript of the revised text.

[4] The total value of the Prothero Bequest in Oct. 1936 was more than £22,400. The Society retained certain articles of library furniture, which had been in Sir George Prothero's home, and holds also his private papers. His lecture notes, pamphlets, press cuttings and some other collections were given to the libraries of the Universities of Edinburgh and London, the National Library of Wales, and the National Portrait Gallery.

housing costs which Council was not prepared to contemplate. It was true that the value of the Prothero Bequest was substantially greater than had at first been anticipated; and the ways in which it could be employed—the promotion of historical research in modern times, the acquisition and maintenance of a library, and other of the Society's purposes —were generously defined. But it was not the primary object of the bequest to relieve the Society's housing problem at the expense of its scholarly activities. Reluctantly Council decided that the Society must seek a less expensive home; the President himself found it a dignified set of rooms in part of the former Lindsey House at 96 Cheyne Walk; and here it moved a few months after his own retirement from the presidency.

What had been the result of the new dispensation begun in 1933? Powicke thought of the Society as a 'clearing house' and a 'meeting place' for scholars. He wished to see it conducting major research enterprises. He hoped that its library would become '*the* centre and home of local record publications'. He dreamt of hundreds of Associates attending its meetings and using its books, of closer relations with the graduate schools of the universities, and of a widening influence and an increasing usefulness in the organization of historical studies.[1] This may have been an over-ambitious programme. But it was the vision of Prothero as seen through the eyes of Powicke. And if the vision could not be realised, nevertheless the Society had been brought back into the mainstream of historical activity. It had been given a 'definite policy' and endowed with a new life. When, at the age of 81, Hubert Hall retired from the Directorship in 1938, to be succeeded by C. R. Cheney and A. V. Judges jointly, the Directors, it was understood, would be responsible, as a general rule, for the production of four volumes each year,

[1] *Transactions*, 4th ser., xvi (1933), pp. 45–53; xx (1937), pp. 1–12.

two in the Camden Series, one of *Transactions* and one in
the Society's other publications;[1] and this programme took
account neither of the *Writings on British History* nor of
those long-term projects in which the Society had an interest—the new edition of Gross, and the eighteenth-century
volume of the *Bibliography of British History*.[2]

There was a moment in 1936 when Powicke thought of
Winston Churchill, who was elected an Honorary Vice-
President in this same year, as his successor. 'You would
get', he wrote, 'very good presidential addresses'.[3] This
would have meant a return to a 'decorative' instead of a working President. But Churchill was reserved to preside over
another enterprise. In the event, one great medievalist, F. M.
Stenton, succeeded another, to hold the presidency for a
second term during the years of the Second World War and
to enrich *Transactions* not with four but with eight notable
addresses.

The war inevitably set back the Society's plans. The ex-
periment, begun in 1938, of holding informal evening dis-
cussions in addition to the ordinary meetings, came to an
end. Several of these last were cancelled. *Transactions*, by
1944, were reduced to a half of their normal size. The flow
of Camden volumes was delayed. The editor of *Writings*
was called up on war-service, and when he returned to
ordinary civilian life became Secretary and Librarian of the
Institute of Historical Research. And the number of Fellows
declined. Yet the Literary Directors managed to produce,
under conditions of great difficulty, seven Camden volumes

---

[1] Minutes, 10 March 1938.

[2] The effective co-operation of the American Historical Association
in the production of this volume was secured by the appointment in
1937 of Stanley Pargellis as joint-editor. The Carnegie Corporation
made a grant of $2,000 in 1942 towards its completion. Minutes,
11 March 1937, 10 Oct. 1942. The volume was published in 1951.

[3] Powicke to Bellot, 6 May 1936. Bellot Papers.

between 1940 and 1945, five of *Transactions* and two in the Guides and Handbooks Series.[1] The Society's receipts in 1944–5 were less than £100 short of those in 1938–9, and Council could still hope, in 1946, to be able to maintain its publishing activities almost at the level anticipated before the war.[2]

How nearly this expectation was realised is evident from the record of the post-war decade covered by the presidencies of R. W. Seton-Watson, T. F. T. Plucknett and H. H. Bellot.[3] Miss Curran, the Society's last link with the very distinguished intellectual circle of Sir George and Lady Prothero, had retired from the Assistant Secretaryship in 1943, and her post was not permanently filled till 1946, when Miss Aileen M. Armstrong came to the Society from the English Place Name Society with the more honorific title of Secretary. The Literary Directorship, meanwhile, had again been united in a single pair of hands, those of Philip Grierson; and during his ten years of office, from 1945 to 1955, Mr Grierson was responsible for the publication of no fewer than thirty-one volumes.[4] Mr Milne, for his part, continued to edit the *Writings on British History*, though heavily engaged in other work.[5] And, as the decade ended, the Society

[1] N. R. Ker's *Medieval libraries of Great Britain* (1941) and C. R. Cheney's *Handbook of dates for students of English history* (1945). There was also one Miscellaneous Publication, the *Domesday Monachorum of Christ Church, Canterbury*, edited by D. C. Douglas in 1944.

[2] Report to Council on the Financial Position of the Society, 18 May 1946.

[3] The Presidential term was altered in 1946, henceforth beginning in December instead of February, the financial year ending in June, and the dates of *Transactions* coinciding with the calendar year.

[4] Including the *Guide to the national and provincial directories of England and Wales, excluding London, published before 1856*, by Jane E. Norton (1950), and the *Handbook of oriental history*, edited by C. H. Philips (1951).

[5] To assist him Mrs Phyllis M. Jacob was appointed as part-time

embarked, together with the American Historical Association, the British Academy and the Medieval Academy of
America, on the ambitious venture of completing and, where
necessary, revising, all the work that had been done during
the last half-century to provide a select bibliography of
British history from medieval to modern times.[1]

This plan embraced the long-contemplated edition of
Gross, on which work had been indefinitely suspended, a
revision of the bibliographies of Tudor and Stuart history,
edited by Conyers Read and Godfrey Davies, the preparation of a nineteenth-century bibliography, and the provision of a back-file of *Writings on British History* for the
years 1901 to 1933. It was made possible by a grant in aid of
$96,000 in 1956 from the Ford Foundation.[2] To the Society
fell the sole responsibility of producing the back-file of
Writings, and this it had almost accomplished by 1968.[3] A
Committee of the Society and the Medieval Academy became responsible for the new edition of Gross; and this also
was nearly ready by 1968.[4] The revised edition of the

Temporary Assistant Officer in May 1952. Earlier assistance had been
provided by Miss Kathleen Edwards and Miss Dora Howard on the
volumes for 1938 and 1939.

[1] Report to the Council of the American Historical Association of
the Committee on Bibliography of British History, and Note by the
Honorary Secretary on the Report of the Committee of the American
Historical Association, 20 Sept. 1952; H. H. Bellot to W. C. Ford,
13 Dec. 1952; Minutes, 11 Oct. 1952, 13 June 1953, 13 Feb. 1954.

[2] Minutes, 14 May 1955; 14 Jan. 1956; 12 May 1956.

[3] See the introduction to vol. i of *Writings on British History, 1901–
1933* (London, 1968). An editorial team was appointed in 1956 with
Miss M. A. Anderson as its head. For the completion of the undertaking after 1961 the Society relied on the devoted services of Professor Bellot, and the series of *Writings* from 1901 to 1945 is, indeed,
a monument to him. For its continuance after 1945 the Institute of
Historical Research assumed the responsibility in 1965.

[4] Edited by Dr Edgar B. Graves.

sixteenth-century bibliography was published in 1959, and, under the direction of an Anglo-American committee, work was still in progress nine years later on the revision of the seventeenth-century volume[1] and on two further volumes covering the years 1789 to 1914.[2]

At this point, in the centenary year of the Society's foundation, it is time to take stock. As in the days of Powicke and Stenton, once again, in the last twelve years, two distinguished medieval scholars, Dom David Knowles and Sir Goronwy Edwards, have added fresh lustre to the presidency. But it is a tribute to the Society's breadth of view that, just as they were preceded by a historian of one part of the western hemisphere, so their successor was a historian of another. The Literary Directorship, whose holders have deserved so well of the Society since Hubert Hall first took office in 1891, has been occupied in turn since 1955 by Professor Denys Hay and Dr Pierre Chaplais, but was again divided between a medievalist and a modernist in 1964. And, in part to relieve the growing burden felt by successive Honorary Secretaries, an Honorary Librarian was appointed for the first time in 1965.

The Society's income, under the fostering care of its Treasurers, has steadily increased.[3] The number of sub-

---

[1] Directed, after the death of Godfrey Davies in 1957, by Dean Mary F. Keeler.

[2] Edited by Professor I. R. Christie and Dr Lucy M. Brown and by Professor H. J. Hanham respectively.

[3] The Society owes an especial debt to Professor T. F. Reddaway, its Honorary Treasurer from June 1949 till his death in October 1967. The benefaction which he made to it of £5,000 in 1966, in memory of his father, W. F. Reddaway, is a memorial both to the father and to the son. Other benefactions made to the Society include, in 1944, the notes and memoranda of Miss E. M. Robinson relating to the books and archives of Alleyn's College of God's Gift and the reversionary bequest of her estate.

scribing libraries has more than doubled since 1945.[1] So has the number of Associates.[2] But the rise in income has failed to keep pace with the rise in prices and in administrative costs. In 1905 the Society could expect to publish one volume of *Transactions* and two Camden volumes at a cost of £400 a year. But £400 paid for one Camden volume only in 1946. It paid for less than a third of a Camden volume in 1968. Subscriptions were raised, for the first time since 1876, in 1949 and again in 1958;[3] and a seven-year covenant scheme was successfully introduced in the following year. These were measures of alleviation. But Council had also to consider the long-term consequences for the Society of a continued inflation and, in particular, the problems with which it would be faced when the tenancy of its rooms in Cheyne Walk expired. The question was even asked whether the Government might not feel some concern for the fate of the learned societies in general and might not be prepared to assist them by finding for them a collective home in central London; and a fruitless enquiry was addressed to the Minister of Public Building and Works. In the event, the Society entered into a mutually advantageous arrangement in 1966 with University College London whereby its library and offices were to be transferred as a separate unit to the shelter of the College, its Fellows and Associates permitted to make use of the College library, and the staff and research students of the College given access to the Society's library.

The move took place in the summer of 1967. Once again the Society's rooms and library are in close proximity to the

---

[1] 305 in 1945, 649 in 1968.

[2] 50 in 1945, 114 in 1968.

[3] From two guineas in 1876 to three in 1950 and four in 1958. The rate for subscribing libraries was £1 in 1897, raised to £1 10s. in 1922, £2 in 1948, £3 in 1953 and £3 10s. in 1958. Compounding for life membership was abolished as from Dec. 1957.

British Museum, the Public Record Office and the Institute of Historical Research. Its members can draw also on the great resources of University College itself. The salary scales of its paid officials have been adjusted to those of the University of London. Its archives have been set in order and its library has been re-arranged. It is ready in the present, as in the past, to defend the interests of historical scholarship wherever or however they may be threatened, whether by the destruction of particular classes of records, the dispersal of manuscripts or the fragmentation of great libraries and museums. Two volumes of centenary essays, selected from *Transactions*, illustrate the extent to which it has acted as a forum for the discussion of some of the significant contributions to historical writing during the last fifty or sixty years;[1] and a *Centenary Guide* to its publications, some four hundred of them in all, if the former Camden volumes are included, is an impressive testimony to the part which it has also played in providing the historian both with the texts which he needs and with those aids to research which become each year more essential.[2] The Society remains the 'principal organization representing English historical scholarship'. But it needs all the support that historians everywhere, whatever specialist label they may attach to themselves, can give it. A Society is something more than the sum of its parts. But if any of the parts are missing, the whole cannot be complete.

[1] *Essays in Medieval History*, edited by R. W. Southern, and *Essays in Modern History*, edited by I. R. Christie (London, 1968).

[2] A. T. Milne, *A Centenary Guide to the Publications of the Royal Historical Society 1868–1968 and of the former Camden Society 1838–1897* (London, 1968).

APPENDIX I

The Camden Society[1]

By Charles Johnson

The Camden Society was born in Westminster, at No. 25 Parliament Street, the printing office of J. B. Nichols, the parliamentary printer, and the home of the Society during the whole of its life, on 15 March 1838 at a meeting presided over by Thomas Amyot, secretary of the Slave Compensation Commission and treasurer of the Society of Antiquaries. There were also present: John Bruce, well known for his work on the state papers; John Payne Collier, whose misdirected enthusiasm for Shakespeare and the Elizabethan dramatists brought him a somewhat unpleasant notoriety; the Rev. Joseph Hunter, historian of south Yorkshire and one of the ablest of the original staff of the Public Record Office; Sir Frederick Madden, Keeper of MSS. at the British Museum; John Bowyer Nichols, antiquary, printer and proprietor of the *Gentleman's Magazine*; Thomas Stapleton, a genealogist whose edition of the Norman exchequer rolls is still our prime authority for the history of Anglo-Norman families; and Thomas Wright, who was to become one of the most prolific of editors of early texts. It was a distinguished company; for each of these names has its paragraph in the *Dictionary of National Biography*. The original plan is ascribed to John Gough Nichols (son of J. B. Nichols),[2] John

[1] From an address delivered on 13 Oct. 1938, *Transactions*, 4th ser., xxii (1940), pp. 23–38. See above p. v. A further discussion of the early history of the Society is provided by F. J. Levy, 'The founding of the Camden Society', *Victorian Studies*, vii (1963–4), pp. 295–305.

[2] He also attended the first meeting.

Bruce and Thomas Wright, who aimed at securing publication in this way for historical books which no publisher would risk.

The moment was propitious, for it was in a period when curiosity as to literary antiquities had reached a height rivalling that attained in the seventeenth century. The second Record Commission had expired, after a parliamentary inquiry, not exactly in the odour of sanctity; but its shortcomings and the criticisms on them had helped to popularize the work both of its more capable members and of their unofficial critics. A Public Record Office, to unify the control of the records and facilitate their use, was being planned, and the Act establishing it was to receive the royal assent in the following August. Nor was private enterprise lagging behind. In this same year 1838 the English Historical Society began its comparatively brief but glorious course with Joseph Stevenson's three volumes, Gildas, Nennius, and Bede's *Historia ecclesiastica*. And the year following it was to issue the first volumes of Kemble's *Codex diplomaticus*. It ended with Hamilton's William of Newburgh in 1856, and its work was carried on by the Rolls Series which began in 1858. The Surtees Society, on the lines of which the Camden Society was planned, began its career in 1834 and happily survives. The Cambridge Camden Society, with rather different aims, was founded in 1839 and still does useful work under the name of the Ecclesiological Society.

The meeting resolved to found a society 'for the publication of Early Historical and Literary Remains' to be called the CAMDEN SOCIETY. The draft rules laid down that the annual subscription was to be £1; that the Society should be governed by a President and a Council of twelve including a Treasurer and a Secretary; and that the annual meeting should be held on Camden's birthday, 2 May, beginning in 1839. It was proposed to publish unedited manuscripts, but scarce printed books might also be selected for re-publication. Copies of each work printed were to be sent to every member, and (an important proviso) the surplus stock was to be offered to the public. Another principle was also laid down which has governed the series ever since: viz., 'That the publications of the Society do all form separate and distinct works without any necessary connection; so that they may be bound and arranged as most agreeable to individual taste.' A reminder of the difference in facilities for communication in the period before Rowland Hill's reforms in 1839 is to be found in the provision that the names of candidates for election be circulated 'to all members residing within the limits of the Threepenny Post' (i.e. residing within 12 miles of the G.P.O.) and to such other members as may so require a week before the date of election.

The first meeting of the new Society was held on the following Thursday, 22 March, and Thursday continued to be the usual day for meetings of the Council then elected. This consisted of the persons who had attended the previous meeting, with the exception of Mr Nichols the printer, and with five new names: Charles Purton Cooper, secretary of the second Record Commission, and author of a once well-known compilation on the Public Records; Thomas Crofton Croker, Irish archaeologist and collector of fairy tales; Sir Thomas Phillipps, owner of the famous Middle Hill library; Edgar Taylor, the translator of *Grimm's Fairy Tales*; and William John Thoms, who published his *Book of the Court* in 1838 and was to found *Notes and Queries* in 1849. Lord Francis Egerton (the 'Lord Leveson Gower' and 'sad poet' of the *Ingoldsby Legends*[1]), a prominent politician and afterwards Earl of Ellesmere, was elected President; John Bruce, Treasurer; and Thomas Wright, Secretary. The auditors

[1] It is curious that R. H. Barham does not appear in the list of members. (C. J.).

were John Herman Merivale and Henry Crabb Robinson, literary barristers, the latter known as the friend of Wordsworth and many others and the author of a famous diary, and Richard Taylor, a printer, and, like Edgar, a member of the celebrated Norwich family.

New members poured in rapidly. Among those recorded in the minute book are John Gage, afterwards John Gage Rokewode, director of the Society of Antiquaries; Henry Hallam; Lord Aberdeen; John Britton, the topographer; Bishop Butler of Lichfield ('Butler of Shrewsbury'); Charles Wentworth Dilke, editor of the *Athenaeum*; Sir Henry Ellis; Lord Holland; Lord Langdale, M.R.; Col. Leake; Charles Lever; Francisque Michel; Sir Robert Peel; Samuel Rogers; William Whewell; the Duke of Sussex; Decimus Burton, architect of the Athenaeum; Peter Cunningham, the editor of Horace Walpole; Isaac D'Israeli; Henry Drury; Charles John Palmer, the historian of Yarmouth; Benjamin Thorpe, the Anglo-Saxon scholar; and Dawson Turner, the Norfolk antiquary and botanist. The Society was already large enough in less than a month for the Council to determine on an edition of 500 copies for the first two volumes, Bruce's *Historie of the arrivall of Edward IV in England* and Payne Collier's edition of Bishop Bale's *Kynge Johan*. By 21 June it was already necessary to make the rule that no new members should be entitled to back parts as soon as the numbers should have reached 480. A printed list was issued on July 10 showing a membership closely approaching 500 and widely representative of Victorian culture. It included (besides those already mentioned) librarians such as Bandinel and Philip Bliss of the Bodleian, and S. R. Maitland of Lambeth; heralds as Sir William Betham, Beltz and Planché; antiquaries like Akerman, Gally Knight, Sir Samuel Meyrick and John Henry Parker; Davies Gilbert and L. B. Larking; Cureton, the Syriac scholar; Joseph Bosworth, Alexander

Dyke and J. O. Halliwell; distinguished foreigners such as
Michelet, Teulet and Lappenberg; Oxford celebrities like
Martin Routh, Tommy Short, Hawkins of Oriel and Scott
(of Liddell and Scott); and other notabilities, including the
archbishop of Canterbury, the bishops of Bath and Wells
and Durham; Milman and John Hill Burton; Robert Southey,
Sir Robert Inglis, Sir Francis Palgrave, Lord Braybrooke,
Serjeant Talfourd, Travers Twiss and the youthful John
Ruskin (he won the Newdigate in 1839). It was proposed
in 1839 that the Queen should be asked to be Patron. Prince
Albert joined the Society in 1843 and remained a member
till his death in 1861.

It was clear by this time that the original edition of 500
would not be large enough to satisfy the demands of prospec-
tive members, so the number of copies to be printed was
raised to 1,000 and arrangements were made for printing
another 500 copies of the volumes already issued. The rules
drafted in March 1839, and approved at the first general meeting, held on 2 May at the Freemasons' Tavern,[1] raised the
limit of membership to 1,000 and before 5 March 1840 it had
been considered necessary to increase the edition to 1,250.
The early and remarkable success of the Society had made its
Council too sanguine, for in 1851 an edition of 750 was considered sufficient and the membership afterwards dropped to
between 300 and 400. In its early years, however, there was
no difficulty in keeping up the numbers. Candidates for
admission were forced to wait their turn for the vacancies
due to death or resignation, and a candidates' book was
instituted a week after the general meeting to determine the
order in which aspirants should be admitted. The pressure
does not seem to have slackened until 1845, and the general
meetings continued to be held at the Freemasons' Tavern

[1] In Great Queen Street, on a site now covered by the Connaught
Rooms.

until 1857, when they were transferred to Messrs Nichols's offices.

The new rules adopted at the meeting enlarged the scope of the Society so as to permit the printing of translations, raised the membership limit to 1,000, and provided for the appointment of a Director who could act as Vice-President. This post was assigned to Thomas Amyot, who held it till his death in 1850. It was no sinecure, since the President, after presiding at the first general meeting, left the Society very much to itself, retiring for reasons of health in 1843. His greatest service was permission to publish the *Egerton Papers*, which were edited by Payne Collier in 1840. The task of taking the chair at the annual meeting and at all Council meetings fell to Amyot until Lord Braybrooke succeeded to the presidency on Lord Francis Egerton's retirement. He took a warm interest in the work and was usually present at Council meetings.[1]

The first question, apart from the routine business of membership and selection of works for publication, to concern the Council was that of copyright. It decided in June 1838 to send copies to the five great libraries, and in March 1839 it was decided that all publications should be entered at Stationers' Hall. Another matter which soon acquired importance was the responsibility of the Society for the opinions of its editors. In May 1839 it was laid down that the Council must see the proofs of each work issued, more especially of the prefaces, and in November at the instance of Charles Purton Cooper definite rules were made to secure this end. Unhappily the Council waived its right of control in particular cases; and it consequently happened that in 1844 fifteen Roman Catholic members of the Society

[1] He presided over the Annual General Meetings during his presidency, but Amyot took the chair at far more Council meetings than did Lord Braybrooke.

protested to the Council against some of the language used in the preface to Wright's 'Suppression Papers' (no. 26). The Council replied by printing a notice disclaiming responsibility. . . . Care was to be taken in future that the rules were enforced. Thus we read under the date 7 May 1857: 'Mr Akerman's introduction to the Privy Purse Expenses of Charles II was laid before the Council and approved—with the substitution of the word "monarch" for "profligate" and "successor" for "flinty-hearted brother" on the last page: which amendment the Secretary was directed to communicate to Mr Akerman.'

One trouble of the new Society arose from the necessity of communicating with country members through the medium of local secretaries. As we have seen, postage was a consideration; and the collection of subscriptions and distribution of volumes could not be cheaply done from headquarters. Some of these were among the most distinguished members of the Society, e.g. Lappenberg at Hamburg and Francisque Michel and afterwards Teulet in Paris. A good deal of book-keeping was necessary, and in 1841 it was resolved to pay £50 *per annum* for clerical assistance to the Treasurer. Moreover, some of the local secretaries were inefficient and failed to remit punctually the subscriptions which they had collected. In 1844 the local secretary for Leicester became a bankrupt, and the Society not only lost the subscriptions in his hands, but had to issue to the Leicester subscribers the volumes to which these subscriptions related. In Edinburgh the secretary wisely applied for leave to transfer the distribution of the volumes to a local bookseller. Subscriptions in arrear were another source of trouble. In 1840 it was necessary to suspend the rule as to ejection of members for non-payment in order to avoid losing so valuable a member as Sir Thomas Phillipps, and in the same year the name of Austen Henry Layard was removed under that rule. The penalty was a severe one, as the Society had then a considerable waiting-list.

In 1842 the London Library applied for a set of the publications and was admitted a member. A special privilege was accorded to the Chetham Library, at Manchester, in 1850. This claimed to be the only English library to which access was absolutely free and unrestricted; and on that ground it was presented with a complete set of the Society's publications, and the gift was afterwards brought up to date. A like liberality was shown in 1854 to the Marylebone Public Library on the application of its Working Men's Committee, and in 1857 to the Westminster Public Library, the 'first free public library in London'. In both these cases copies were given of all publications of which more than 50 copies were in stock. The early success of the Society as compared with its reduced numbers in later years, and the consequent excessive editions printed, had caused an accumulation of stock which made it politic to be very liberal to a possible permanent subscriber.

The Society played an honourable part in the agitation to secure access for literary inquirers to early wills. A volume of these was planned in 1848; but the officers of the Prerogative Court refused any facilities, though no difficulty was made at Lambeth with regard to the wills preserved there. A memorial was therefore submitted in 1852 to the Ecclesiastical Courts Commission, setting forth, amongst other things, that 'The authorities of the Prerogative Office in Doctors' Commons perhaps stand alone in their total want of sympathy with literature and in their exclusion of literary enquirers by stringent rules, harshly, and in some cases offensively enforced.'

The attack was renewed in 1854, when Lord Strangford, who was a probable member of the select committee concerned, undertook to raise the question of the custody of old wills. In 1858, in consequence of the coming into force of the Court of Probate Act, conditions improved; and when in 1862 the Society applied to Sir Cresswell Cresswell[1] for leave to print some of the wills from Doctors' Commons, it was granted with the concession also that literary inquirers would in future be permitted to consult all wills previous to the year 1700. In 1864 the Society successfully applied for the extension to the district registries of this ruling; and in 1869 it protested against the proposed imposition of fees for literary searches among wills. In February 1877 it applied, at the same time as the Society of Antiquaries, for the extension of the date to 1760, a privilege which was immediately granted. It also in 1865 successfully advocated the use of photography for making facsimiles of wills.[2]

In 1862 the Society proposed to petition the chancellor of the exchequer for the printing of the rest of the pipe rolls of Henry II; but as a result of informal inquiries at Rolls House made by Charles Purton Cooper the plan was dropped. The Pipe Roll Society, which has now[3] happily completed that portion of its task, was founded in 1883.

Of the literary work of the Society it is . . . almost superfluous to speak. We owe to it so many works which are part of the furniture of our minds, the familiar tools of the historical workshop . . . and though the importance of the volumes varies greatly, it is fair to say that the Society attained its object, and brought within the reach of scholars a series of texts of the highest historical and literary value which would otherwise have remained unpublished as being commercially unprofitable. We may further claim that its

[1] Sir Cresswell Cresswell had become in 1858 first judge in ordinary of the Probate and Divorce Court.

[2] The wording of this paragraph has been amended.

[3] 1938. The series for Henry II was completed in 1930.

activities gave a stimulus to other societies of later foundation which continued the work it had begun, and thus enabled it to restrict its action to that definitely historical field which the Camden Series now occupies . . .[1]

In the early years of the Society its literary side, represented by Payne Collier, Wright and Dyce, was almost as important as its historical, upheld by Bruce, Stapleton and Hunter. But the foundation of the Percy Society in 1840 and the Shakespeare Society in 1841 took away a great part of the pressure in this direction. The Camden Society's outstanding contribution is Albert Way's edition of the *Promptorium parvulorum*, one of the earliest works projected by the Society but only completed in 1865, the year after the foundation by Dr Furnivall of the Early English Text Society. The delay in its production and that of Le Roux de Lincy's *Blonde of Oxford* was a source of perennial anxiety to the Council. The publication of the complementary glossaries, Levins's *Manipulus vocabulorum* (1867), edited by Wheatley, and Herrtage's edition of the *Catholicon* (1881), was undertaken jointly by the two societies.

The problem of dealing with pieces too short to form a volume presented itself at an early stage. The rules of the Society demanded that each work should be separate, with its own title-page and index (if necessary), so that subscribers could arrange and bind their volumes according to any plan which suited them. The plan adopted in 1846 was to issue a number of such separate parts in the same cloth

---

[1] In recognition of William Camden's work as a herald the Society in 1849 embarked on the printing of his Visitations, beginning with the *Visitation of the County of Huntingdon*. The expense of the necessary engraving was in all probability one reason why the Camden Society published no more. Fortunately the Harleian Society, founded in 1870, took on responsibility for such publications and has printed many heraldic Visitations.

cover, leaving the owner free to break up the volume and bind its contents in any order desired. The first volume appeared in the following year . . .

A good many works were suggested for publication and declined. Some were found to be printed already, or to be so similar in character to existing publications as not to deserve print. But some seem to have been rejected on inadequate grounds. Thus Baker's 'History of St John's College, Cambridge' was thought in 1840 to be too local in its interest. Other unsuccessful proposals were Horsley's 'Britannia Romana' and the 'Gesta Romanorum' (1842), the correspondence of Count Koenigsmarck and Sophia Dorothea (1852), and Smith's 'Lives of the Berkeleys' (1855). Herd's metrical chronicle of Edward IV, Edward V, Richard III and Henry VII was refused in 1866 as being more suitable for the Rolls Series (begun in 1858). It never found a place there, but was privately printed for the Roxburghe Club in 1868. Gairdner's *Paston Letters*, offered in 1868, was rightly considered saleable in the ordinary course of trade. In 1870 Eyton offered his *Court of Henry II* but under conditions as to date of publication, which the Society was unable to accept. It also was published through the trade in 1878. M. D. Davis offered 'Documents relating to the early history of the Jews in England' in 1877, but never published a book with that title.[1] 'The Master of Game', proposed by Sir Henry Dryden in 1855 and still unfinished in 1882, was then passed on to the Early English Text Society. Luttrell's Diary, which was proposed in 1855, on the strength of Macaulay's frequent use of it, was found to have been already undertaken by the Clarendon Press. A proposal in 1845 by Dr Giles for a catalogue of English literary and historical manuscripts in Belgium came to nothing because the Society could not offer anything more than the cost of printing. A

[1] Davis published his *Hebrew Deeds of English Jews* in 1888. (C. J.).

suggestion by Marchegay for a volume of documents relating to England in Anjou was refused in the previous year. Another unrealized project was to have a profound effect on the fortunes of the Society. In 1855, when about 60 volumes had been issued, it was proposed to compile a general index to the publications of the first twenty years on the lines of that made by Henry Gough for the Parker Society; and the proposal was renewed three years later, and the cost estimated at £200. The question remained open till 1868 when the hundredth volume was in sight, and £500 was then assigned for the purpose and Mr Gough's services were engaged. In 1874, after six years' work, the compiler was hopeful of being able to go to press with an index to the 105 volumes of the original series. In 1879, however, the task was still unfinished, and a committee was appointed to report on it. The compiler had then been paid £400 on account, had completed the slips, and had revised A and part of B. The remainder of the alphabet was sorted to the first letter only. It was decided to print 500 copies, but Mr Gough, who was in failing health, begged to be released from his task. The completed part of the index (A–Baudouin) was issued in sheets in 1881, but, as the Society could neither find a new indexer nor the funds to pay him and print the index, the plan was definitely abandoned in the same year. It had exhausted the reserve funds, and henceforth the Society lived from hand to mouth.

The Society was fortunate in its officers. Its second President, Lord Braybrooke, was diligent in his attendance at both Council and general meetings till his health began to fail in 1856. On his death in 1858, Earl Jermyn, afterwards Marquess of Bristol, succeeded, and remained till his death in 1864. The Marquess Camden presided for less than two years. On his death in 1866, Sir William Tite, architect of the Royal Exchange, was elected President, and took an active part in the business, dying just before the general meeting of 1873, which was on that account postponed. His successor, the Earl of Verulam, also attended Council meetings, but resigned in 1887. The Earl of Crawford, owner of the famous library at Haigh Hall, was elected in 1888, and remained President until the dissolution of the Society. The Directors were Thomas Amyot (1839–50), John Bruce (1850–69) and Samuel Rawson Gardiner (1869–97); the Treasurers, John Bruce (1838–45), John Payne Collier (1845–61), William Henry Blaauw (1861–5), William Chappell, the musical antiquary (1865–81) and James Joel Cartwright, secretary of the Public Record Office (1882–97); the Secretaries, Thomas Wright (March–November 1838), William John Thoms (1838–72), Alfred Kingston of the Public Record Office (1872–85) and James Gairdner (1885–97).

Among the minor matters which concerned the Council we may record the great controversy on spelling in 1867. A correspondent of the *Athenaeum* complained that the spelling of Bargrave's *Pope Alexander the Seventh and the College of Cardinals* had been modernized, and the savour of the work destroyed. F. J. Furnivall (who may be suspected of having written this letter) brought the matter before the general meeting on 2 May with a motion that 'in the Society's books the spelling of the original documents be preserved, and that contractions be extended in italics'. The motion was, however, ultimately withdrawn.

Trouble also arose from A. J. Horwood's *Commonplace Book of John Milton*, issued in 1876, which contained a number of errors due to haste and bad proof-reading; but Mr Horwood replaced this defective edition by a corrected one in the following year at his own expense: an act of generosity which the Society was in no position to refuse.

It is interesting to note the rise and fall of literary newspapers, as shown by the instructions for sending out review copies. These were sent in 1854 to *The Times, Chronicle, Athenaeum, Examiner, Literary Gazette*, and to *Frazer's* and *Blackwood's* magazines. In 1861 an advertisement for new members was sent to *The Times, Morning Post, Athenaeum, Saturday Review* and *Notes and Queries*. In 1867 the *Pall Mall Gazette* is added to the list. In 1874 the review copies go to *The Times, Standard, Pall Mall Gazette, Athenaeum, Saturday Review, Academy, Spectator* and *Notes and Queries*.

The financial troubles of the Society arose, in a manner, from its early success, which raised the output to 1,250 copies in 1840, and made it necessary for the Treasurer in 1841 to have a grant of £50 per annum for clerical assistance. When the numbers dropped to 300 or 400 the output and overhead expenses could not at once be proportionately reduced, and accumulations of stock required warehouse room which had to be paid for in one shape or another. As early as 1850 the Council began to be uneasy at the cost of unexpected appendices, and required that estimates should be submitted. In 1853 some of the surplus stock was sold to Mr Stevens at about sixpence a volume. Further economies were attempted in 1858, when the Society decided to buy its own paper, and in 1859 the printing expenses were reconsidered. Messrs Nichols agreed to accept a reduction of 5s. per sheet, but declined an offer of 7s. 6d. to cover corrections on the ground that the average cost in a recent volume had been over 9s. The stock held numbered 8,300, and it was agreed that, in consideration of the reduction, the Society should pay £5 per annum warehouse rent and do its own insurance. The Council ordered that editors were not to have more than two revises. In 1860 it was suggested by the printers that new members be offered sets of all volumes in print for £15, or a choice of 25 volumes for £5, but the Council preferred to continue its existing offer of half-price. In 1868 there was a fire at the printers', and the Society claimed £114 3s. od.

for insurance. A report was made on the financial position in 1881, which showed that the Society had only 43 life and 183 paying members, and that careful estimates of cost were imperative. In the following month the Treasurer resigned. Means were already so straitened that Pauli's proposal of the Wardrobe Accounts of Henry, Earl of Derby, could not be accepted. This was in 1879, and Pauli died soon afterwards. The book was afterwards undertaken by Stubbs, who gave it up on accepting a bishopric in 1884, and was finally issued[1] jointly with the East and West Prussian Historical Society in 1894, the German edition edited by Dr Prutz and the English by Miss Lucy Toulmin Smith. In 1892 there had been a slight recovery, there being 28 life-members and 237 subscribers of whom 118 were libraries, and an effort was made to attract more libraries. In 1894 it was reported that the irrecoverable arrears of subscribers amounted to £95, but that the Society could still carry on for a while. It was unable, however, to issue more than one volume a year after this date.

In 1896 it was suggested that if the Society would amalgamate with the Royal Historical Society, which had approached it ten years before on the subject of the Domesday Celebration, the combined membership would be large enough to support the burden of two Camden volumes and one of the Royal Historical Society's proceedings. A committee was appointed to consider this and reported favourably on 11 March 1896. It consisted of Sir Mountstuart Grant Duff, Frederic Harrison, Robert Hovenden (Treasurer), and Hubert Hall (Director and Secretary) on behalf of the Royal Historical Society, and of S. R. Gardiner, J. J. Cartwright, James Gairdner and J. Silvester Davies for the Camden Society. A circular was issued to the members on

[1] *Expeditions to Prussia and the Holy Land, made by Henry, Earl o, Derby.* Camden Society, new series, lii. (C. J.).

2 May 1896 embodying these proposals. In November 1896 it was stipulated that three members of the Council of the Camden Society should be nominated to serve on that of the Royal Historical Society; and on 19 November the Royal Historical Society adopted the plan, which was confirmed at a special general meeting of the Camden Society on 2 December. At a final Council meeting on 28 April 1897, arrangements were made for clearing the Camden Society's liabilities, and a special request was made that the Royal Historical Society should not dispose of the Camden Society's stock at lower prices than those already fixed by the Council. The Camden Society issued as its last volume in 1897, vol. iii of *The Nicholas Papers*, and passed peacefully out of existence on 1 May 1897 . . . [1]

[1] Since 1897 the initials 'C. S.' have continued to appear on volumes of texts issued by the Royal Historical Society, but they have signified Camden Series instead of Camden Society.

APPENDIX II

Officers of the Royal Historical Society

PRESIDENTS

George Grote	6 Jan.	1870–18 June	1871†
John, 1st Earl Russell (Lord John Russell)	23 Nov.	1871–28 May	1878†
Henry Austin Bruce, 1st Baron Aberdare	13 June	1878–19 Feb.	1891
Sir Mountstuart Elphinstone Grant Duff	{ 19 Feb. { 21 Feb.	1891–21 Feb. 1895–16 Feb.	1895 1899
Adolphus William Ward[1]	20 April	1899–20 Mar.	1901
George Walter Prothero[2]	21 March	1901–16 Feb.	1905
The Rev. William Hunt	16 Feb.	1905–18 Feb.	1909
The Ven. William Cunningham	18 Feb.	1909–20 Feb.	1913
Charles Harding Firth[3]	20 Feb.	1913–15 Feb.	1917
Charles William Chadwick Oman[4]	15 Feb.	1917–10 Feb.	1921
The Hon. John William Fortescue[5]	10 Feb.	1921–12 Feb.	1925
Thomas Frederick Tout	12 Feb.	1925–14 Feb.	1929
Sir Richard Lodge	14 Feb.	1929– 9 Feb.	1933
Frederick Maurice Powicke[6]	9 Feb.	1933–11 Feb.	1937
Frank Merry Stenton[7]	{ 11 Feb. { 15 Feb.	1937–15 Feb. 1941–10 Feb.	1941 1945
Robert William Seton-Watson	10 Feb.	1945–11 Dec.	1948
Theodore Frank Thomas Plucknett	11 Dec.	1948–13 Dec.	1952
Hugh Hale Bellot	13 Dec.	1952– 8 Dec.	1956
The Rev. Michael Clive Knowles (Dom David Knowles)	8 Dec.	1956–10 Dec.	1960
Sir (John) Goronwy Edwards	10 Dec.	1960–12 Dec.	1964
Robert Arthur Humphreys	12 Dec.	1964– 6 Dec.	1968
Richard William Southern	6 Dec.	1968–	

[1] Kt., 1913.
[2] K.B.E., 1920.
[3] Kt., 1922.
[4] K.B.E., 1920.
[5] K.C.V.O., 1926.
[6] Kt., 1946.
[7] Kt., 1948.

PRESIDENTS (OR CHAIRMEN) OF COUNCIL

George Harris	13 Jan.	1876–11 May 1876
George Harris ⎫ Benjamin Ward Richardson[1] ⎭	11 May	1876– 9 Nov. 1876
B. W. Richardson	9 Nov.	1876–11 July 1878
James Heywood	14 Nov.	1878– 6 Dec. 1880
Gustavus George Zerffi	6 Dec.	1880–19 March 1885
Oscar Browning	19 March 1885–15 March 1888
Charles Alan Fyffe	15 March 1888–19 April 1888
Oscar Browning	15 May	1888–16 Oct. 1894

TREASURERS

Henry Wright[2]	❦ 23 Nov.	1868–1869 (n.d.)
Alfred Gliddon[3]	6 Jan.	1870–12 Nov. 1874
William Herbage	27 May	1875–21 Oct. 1892†
Robert Hovenden[4]	17 Nov.	1892–29 Sept. 1904
H. R. Tedder	20 Oct.	1904– 8 Aug. 1924†
Charles Johnson	23 Oct.	1924–13 March 1930
F. J. C. Hearnshaw	13 March 1930–11 June 1931
M. S. Giuseppi	11 June	1931– 9 Feb. 1939
M. H. I. Letts	9 Feb.	1939–11 June 1949
T. F. Reddaway	11 June	1949–26 Oct. 1967†
G. R. C. Davis	10 Nov.	1967–

LITERARY DIRECTORS

The Rev. Charles Rogers (Historiographer)	23 Nov.	1868– 5 Jan. 1881
Hubert Hall	19 March 1891–31 Oct. 1938

[1] Kt., 1893.

[2] There is no evidence that Wright ever exercised the functions of Treasurer or of when he resigned the office.

[3] F. B. Kirby, who had been Vice-Treasurer and then Assistant-Treasurer since 24 Feb. 1871, was Acting-Treasurer from 12 Nov. 1874 to 27 May 1875.

[4] E. M. Lloyd was Acting-Treasurer from 29 Sept. 1904 to 20 Oct. 1904.

C. R. Cheney⎱	⎰31 Oct.	1938–10 March 1945
A. V. Judges ⎰	⎱31 Oct.	1938– 1 Nov. 1945
Philip Grierson	1 Nov.	1945– 1 Oct. 1955
Denys Hay	1 Oct.	1955–30 June 1958
P. T. V. M. Chaplais	1 July	1958– 1 Oct. 1964
G. W. S. Barrow⎱		
I. R. Christie ⎰	1 Oct.	1964–

SECRETARIES AND HONORARY SECRETARIES
1868–1894

L. C. Alexander (Secretary)	23 Nov.	1868–6 Jan. 1870 [?]
T. L. Kington-Oliphant (Hon. Secretary)	6 Jan.	1870–1872 (n.d.)
The Rev. Charles Rogers (Hon. Secretary)	26 Nov.	1872–11 Nov. 1875
(Secretary)	11 Nov.	1875– 5 Jan. 1881
William Herbage (Hon. Secretary)	5 Jan.	1881–16 March 1882
P. E. Dove (Secretary)	16 March	1882–21 Nov. 1894†

HONORARY SECRETARIES SINCE 1894

Hubert Hall	30 Nov.	1894– 1 Oct. 1903
H. E. Malden	1 Oct.	1903–16 March 1931†
F. J. C. Hearnshaw	14 May	1931– 8 Feb. 1934
H. H. Bellot	8 Feb.	1934–13 Dec. 1952
R. A. Humphreys	12 Dec.	1953–10 Dec. 1955
R. W. Greaves	10 Dec.	1955– 8 March 1958
Alun Davies	10 May	1958–14 Oct. 1961
F. R. H. Du Boulay	14 Oct.	1961– 1 Sept. 1965
J. H. Burns	1 Sept.	1965–

CLERKS, ASSISTANT SECRETARIES AND SECRETARIES SINCE 1894

Thomas Mason (Clerk)	20 Dec.	1894–16 May 1901
Miss M. B. Curran (Clerk)	16 May	1901–21 May 1903
(Assistant Secretary)	21 May	1903–15 May 1943
Miss C. Jamison (Assistant Secretary)	24 June	1943–24 June 1946

Miss A. M. A. E. Armstrong		
(Secretary)	24 June	1946–
Miss J. L. Austen (Clerk)	25 Feb.	1946–12 Jan. 1952
Miss P. Warren (Clerk)	18 Feb.	1952–18 July 1953
Miss S. P. Butcher (Clerk)	13 Aug.	1953–26 Feb. 1955
Mrs. M. D. C. Gallop		
(Assistant Secretary)	30 May	1955–

HONORARY LIBRARIAN

A. T. Milne   1 Sept. 1965–

LIBRARIANS

W. E. Poole	14 Jan.	1875–1877 (n.d.)
The Rev. Thomas Hunter	8 Nov.	1877–1879 (n.d.)
W. S. W. Vaux	13 Nov.	1879–1882 [?]
W. E. Poole	Nov.	1882 [?]–1890 [?]
Thomas Mason	19 May	1892–16 May 1901
Miss M. B. Curran	16 May	1901–15 May 1943
Miss C. Jamison	24 June	1943–24 June 1946
Miss A. M. A. E. Armstrong	24 June	1946–

ASSISTANT OFFICER AND JUNIOR LIBRARIAN

A. T. Milne   13 June 1935– 1 Jan.   1946